T0002481

Three Plays

THE
SEAGULL
LIBRARY OF
GERMAN
LITERATURE

Three Plays

PHILOCTETES, THE HORATIAN, MAUSER

HEINER MÜLLER

TRANSLATED BY NATHANIEL MCBRIDE

WITH AN INTRODUCTION BY UWE SCHÜTTE

LONDON NEW YORK CALCUTTA

This publication has been supported by a grant from
the Goethe-Institut India

Seagull Books, 2019

Philoktet (from Werke 3 Die Stücke 1)
Die Horatier / Mauser (from Werke 4 Die Stücke 2—in one volume)
© Suhrkamp Verlag, Frankfurt am Main, 2000

First published in English by Seagull Books, 2011

ISBN 978 0 8574 2 708 3

British Library Cataloguing-in-Publication Data
A catalogue record for this book is available from the British Library

Typeset by Seagull Books, Calcutta, India
Printed and bound by WordsWorth India, New Delhi, India

CONTENTS

ACKNOWLEDGEMENTS

The translator would like to express his thanks
to Isabel Cole and Tom Morrison for their help
and advice with this text.

INTRODUCTION

These three plays, written only a little over 40 years ago, seem to come from a world very different from our own. They were written in a country that no longer exists, and for a kind of theatre that would scarcely seem possible today. Their subject is the historical past, but a past viewed with an eye to its relevance to the present, a past that still holds discoveries that might transform life as it is now lived—and not, as seems so often the case today, merely confirm it. Their relation to theatrical tradition itself is also different, treating it as living thing, to be developed and critiqued, rather than as a dead canon, to be quoted and pastiched. And behind all this lies a fundamental presupposition of art's ability to act upon and change the social world, and the power of theatre as a political institution.

At the same time, they stand on the brink of the dissolution of all those assumptions, and register, perhaps unconsciously, their approaching collapse. The developments they make to the theatrical tradition are equally symptoms of its disintegration, while the subjects they address have for us today the curious quality of seeming both vitally important and impossibly remote—remote not so much because their dilemmas have been resolved but because they have been tacitly accepted as intractable. Their common theme of political violence is treated cynically today, as something that everyone 'knows' to be always wrong in principle but, given the imperfect nature of the world, indispensible in practice. These plays were written at a time when some, at least, were less willing to accept such contradictory conclusions. They reveal not so much how we have moved on from this question as retreated from it.

Their author was a German playwright whose life was, as he put it, 'intruded upon' very early on by some of the better-known catastrophes of European history. Heiner Müller (1929–95) lived most of his life under two dictatorships, growing up under the Nazi one, and then coming of age and making his career under its Communist successor. In his autobiography he recalls that one of his earliest memories was of the arrest of his father by the Gestapo; through a gap in his bedroom door, the four-year-old Müller watched his father being beaten up and taken away, something he describes as a 'key scene' for the work that would follow. It also perhaps played a role in his decision to remain in East Germany after the rest of his family had emigrated. This was, he later claimed, a consciously political decision, and made with few illusions; though the East German regime was clearly a dictatorship, it was also, as he put it, 'a dictatorship against the people who had damaged my childhood'. It was by no means certain that it would actually build a better society but it was at least an instance of 'the new bad . . . and that was better than the familiar old. That was my position at the time.'

It was a precarious position, not least because the dictatorship had little patience for ambiguous, let alone critical, support. But it was probably not Müller's only reason for staying; equally important to him must have been the presence in the new state of the dramatist Bertolt Brecht (1898–1956), who had returned after the war to settle in East Berlin. Brecht's influence on Müller's work cannot be overestimated; much of what he wrote is concerned with developing the new dramatic forms devised by the older playwright. Müller's earliest plays are a series of attempts to combine Brechtian methods with the socialist realist aesthetics prescribed by the new Communist state. Even at this stage, however, a tension between the two is detectable. For Brecht's concept of drama was inherently critical; it aimed at getting audiences to examine, reflect on, and imagine alternatives to what they saw on stage. Socialist realism, by contrast, at least as it was understood by the East German authorities, was essentially an affirmative aesthetic, concerned with holding up examples for its audiences to admire and emulate. Müller's early 'production plays', which deal with the difficulties of building socialism in the German Democratic Republic, embody this tension. The challenges they portray—acute material shortages, widespread cynicism and despair, and a working class profoundly distrustful of authorities claiming to govern in their name—seem almost insurmountable, while the solutions they arrive at are only too clearly imperfect and unstable. *Der Lohndrücker* (*The Scab*, 1957), his first major play, has as its hero the stock socialist realist figure of the model factory worker whose example inspires his workmates to meet the production plan. Halfway through, however, it is revealed that the same hero worked just as enthusiastically for a Nazi munitions firm during the war, drastically undermining the 'moral example' he sets. Müller's next play, *Korrektur* (*Correction*, 1958), went even further, showing an honest Party official who falls foul of corrupt working practices in the building industry. The work was heavily criticized and Müller was forced to rewrite the text before its performance would be permitted. However, it was his third play, *Die Umsiedlerin* (*The Resettler*, 1961), a comedy about the government's land reform policy, that evidently persuaded the authorities its author had gone too far and needed to be made an example of. Accused of 'counter-revolutionary and anti-Communist tendencies', it was closed down after its opening night, and its actors, director and author forced to perform public self-criticisms. Müller himself was expelled from the Writers' Union, placing him under an effective ban from publishing or staging any of his work.

There followed several years of financial hardship and professional isolation, during which his efforts to get his work back on stage or in print were repeatedly frustrated. It was also a time of personal tragedy; after his next major play, *Der Bau* (*The Building Site*, 1966) was rejected from the theatre, Müller's wife and collaborator Inge took her own life. The three plays in this volume come from this time. In certain respects they develop themes already present in the earlier works, but in a more obvious way they mark a decisive break with them. They replace the contemporary settings of the 'production plays' with archaic and mythical ones, and their robust demotic dialogue with an archaic language set in rhythmic verse. Perhaps the most important change, though, is in their dramatic form, for in these works Müller returned to the *Lehrstück*, or learning play, a radical kind of political theatre developed by Brecht 40 years earlier.

All Brecht's theatre sought to instigate social change, but none more emphatically than the *Lehrstück*. It stood, so to speak, in the vanguard of his 'non-Aristotelean theatre' which aimed at instilling among audiences a critical consciousness of what they saw on stage by rejecting one of the most basic devices of western theatre, the manipulation of the audience's empathy for its characters. Actors were encouraged not to associate themselves with the parts they played but to 'alienate' themselves from them: to depict rather than embody their characters, to quote their lines rather than enact them. It was a theatre that worked by breaking the spell of the theatre, revealing 'its own device' in order to direct audiences' attention from the fortunes of the individual characters to sober and critical reflection upon their actions. To facilitate this, Brecht would divide the action of his plays into discontinuous scenes, so that the stages of its narrative could be separately analyzed and examined. The result was a drama not of seamless flow but of discontinuity and interruption, a drama of component parts which could be taken out, modified and put back together again like the parts of an engine.

The *Lehrstück* took these methods and applied them to the presentation of overtly political and social themes, producing an extremely stark and rigorous kind of theatrical text from which everything extraneous had been stripped. The result has frequently been misunderstood as, in Jonathan Kalb's words, a 'heavy-handed form of ideological indoctrination'. In fact, the *Lehrstück* was anything but this: rather than telling its audiences what to think, it offered a practical means for working out their own thoughts and attitudes towards the subjects it presented. Its central innovation was the rejection of the traditional division of theatre into actors and audience. For a *Lehrstück* is a play written first and foremost for performers, not spectators, and the opportunities for learning that it offers require an active involvement. Players were supposed to rehearse, perform and discuss its text in a kind of 'master class', with different performers taking up different roles at different times, and all of them discussing changes and revisions to the text where necessary. As Brecht put it, what a *Lehrstück* had to teach was 'learnt by performing, not watching it'. Performances were in fact of secondary importance, and need not take place at all. The Lehrstück required neither an audience nor a theatre, and indeed was often conceived for use in schools and educational institutes, where its producers would also be those who consumed it.

It was to this collectivist, participatory, radically democratic form of theatre that Müller turned at a time when his plays had been all but banned from the stage. If there was a deliberate irony in this, there was also a deliberate purpose: we may imagine that the very 'impossibility' of staging such plays made them interesting to him; not only for what it revealed about the society in which he lived but also about the very possibility of political theatre itself. Reviving Brecht's devices meant reassessing and critiquing them, as his note at the end of *Mauser* makes clear: the three plays are 'an experimental series' that aims to 'examine/criticize Brecht's theory and practice of the *Lehrstücke*'.

Written in the late 1920s and early 30s, Brecht's plays were concerned with the critique of bourgeois society and the need to struggle against it. Müller's, by contrast, written 40 years later, have as their subject the actual societies that struggle brought into being. Brecht was writing in the aftermath of the October Revolution and the possibilities for social and political transformation that it seemed to open up, Müller with the knowledge of how far those possibilities had been disappointed and betrayed as well as of the crimes and atrocities committed in their name. So while Brecht wrote in a context of historical opportunity, Müller's was one of missed historical chances. This, as he would later make clear in an interview, had profound consequences for theatre and its practice:

> '[. . .] when the chances are missed, what was a plan for a new world begins differently anew—as a dialogue with the dead. [. . .] Against the background of world history, for which communism is a requirement, the dialogue stands for a freeing of the past.'

Brecht's *Lehrstücke*, with their 'plan for a new world', spoke directly to the future; Müller's, by contrast, are forced to pursue this task more obliquely, by turning first to the past. Only by coming to terms with it can another route be found out of the dead end of the present. But for this, a very different approach to Brecht's pragmatic, common-sense, matter-of-fact rationalism is required. A 'dialogue with the dead' demands an engagement with the irrational, with magic, incantation and ritual, with dream and nightmare, with paradox and irresolvable contradiction. All of these are to be found in Müller's *Lehrstücke*, but perhaps the first paradox to note is the one between the very form and content of the plays themselves. The *Lehrstück* form presupposed conditions of free and open debate among its performers; Müller's works combine this with a content that was, at the time of writing, politically taboo. This constitutive 'impossibility' of the plays exposes a fundamental contradiction between the emancipatory claims and repressive reality of the societies of 'real existing socialism'. It has another consequence as well: since the subject of the plays cannot be discussed openly, they must assume the form of allegory, an element that was absent from Brecht's original *Lehrstücke*. The *Lehre* or lesson of Müller's plays is allegorical in form because the practical models of behaviour they offer can only be grasped by the proper understanding of history. And this is so because the present can no longer be made sense of in its own terms; it is a fabric of lies and obfuscations, whose true meaning lies buried in the past.

The other striking difference of Müller's plays is their hermeticism. Brecht's works were designed for ease of use: their rigorous, machine-like structure aimed at serving the needs of their performer-users, enabling them to be dismantled and reconstructed at will. Müller's plays preserve and develop this mechanical quality but in a quite different direction: rather than useful tools, they are more like powerful but self-enclosed mechanisms, of a kind that exclude the intrusion of any human agency. The compulsive, driving rhythms of *The Horatian* and *Mauser* are machinery that threaten to entrap their performers rather than contraptions they might adapt for their own use. The play texts themselves are awkward and angular; far from lending themselves to being performed, they if anything operate by resisting their own staging. Conflict is thus in a certain sense shifted from within the text to between text and the physical stage itself; as Müller puts it, the 'translation of text into theatre' should be 'a test of endurance for the participants . . . the body's struggle against the violence of the expediency of ideas'. While Brecht's plays tend to integrate text and actual performance, making the one open and adaptable to the other, Müller's insist on their incompatibility. Although his note to *Mauser* concludes with detailed suggestions for how the play might be performed, a more accurate description of how he 'envisaged' its performance might be the one he gave in a late interview:

> *Mauser* was the first time that I didn't have the slightest idea how it was going to be done on stage. Not the remotest idea. There was a text, and in my imagination there was no space, no stage, no actors for this text, nothing. [. . .] I mean, basically these are plays or texts only for staging inside my brain or my head. They're performed inside this skull.

Here the collective unity of the *Lehrstück* group of committed activist-players is supplanted by the isolated unity of the author's individual mind, in what appears as an extreme inversion of Brecht's original intentions. The space for revolutionary praxis has shrunk to the interior of the skull, producing a *Lehrstück* that is a kind of negative of itself, enclosed, uncanny and sinister.

It would be a mistake, though, to read these plays as a

simple turn towards defeat and despair. Their various mutations—the turn towards allegory, the revival of archaic themes and forms, the growing hermeticism of the texts— are better seen as the outcome of a rigorous test of endurance to which Müller subjected the *Lehrstück*, one aimed at determining whether a genuinely political theatre could still survive in the extremely hostile circumstances in which he wrote. It is a test that places the plays under a high degree of formal tension, a tension that seems constantly to threaten them with an implosion that would turn them into the opposite of what they were supposed to mean. But the tension is also necessary to the clear, consistent and logically developed series of political lessons they aim to convey; without it, without registering the near impossibility of their own existence, they can communicate nothing. For as I hope will become clear, the content of those lessons is consistently idealist, in the best sense of the word. All three plays are essentially a series of reflections upon the legacy of Stalinism and a set of proposals for a politics that would combat it, a politics calling for pragmatism mixed with idealism, for an open debate about the crimes of the past, and for the retrieval of a genuinely revolutionary ethics from its association with the atrocities of the past. It is a politics that, above all, requires a radical reconception of what it means to be human, together with a rejection of the Humanism that had been central to so much of the Left's thinking in the twentieth century.

Philoctetes, the first of the series, was written over a period of six years, from 1958 to 1964, and partially predates Müller's fall from grace. It is based on a tragedy by

Sophocles, whose subject was an incident from the Trojan war. On the journey out to Troy, Philoctetes saves the Greek fleet from shipwreck by sustaining a serpent's bite. But the poison from the wound leaves him consumed by ravaging pain, and his cries prevent the Greeks from appeasing the gods through sacrifice. To save the mission, Odysseus, the expedition's leader, decides to have him marooned on a barren island. Ten years later, with the Trojan war still raging, the Greeks realize that they will not be victorious without the help of Philoctetes' followers. Odysseus therefore returns to the island, accompanied by Achilles' son Neoptolemos, to persuade the man he had abandoned to follow him back to Troy.

This is the starting point for Müller's play, whose dramatic interest essentially resides in the question of whether its three protagonists will be able to overcome their respective mortal hatred to unite in the common interest of leaving the island together. Neoptolemos, the young idealist, wavers between his commitment to the mission and his ethical qualms about the methods it uses, a dilemma complicated by his personal loathing for Odysseus. Philoctetes, embittered and driven half-mad by his years of isolation, is torn between his desire to escape the life-in-death of exile and his desire to exact revenge on the people who put him there. In this situation, Odysseus, as cynical pragmatist, aims to coordinate these two antagonistic positions to achieve a peaceful resolution that will serve a higher political aim. Several times in course of the play, the possibility of this emerges, only to retreat again; Odysseus' skilful machinations are frustrated each time, either by Neoptolemos' naive sense of personal honour or by Philoctetes' obduracy. Eventually the

confrontation ends in catastrophe. Moved by pity, Neoptolemos returns Philoctetes the bow he has stolen from him,
leaving both him and Odysseus at the latter's mercy. As
Philoctetes prepares to kill Odysseus, Neoptolemos realizes
he can only save himself and the mission by killing the man
he pities to defend the one he loathes.

At first sight it might seem that the lesson of this
Lehrstück is the necessity for Odysseus' clear-sighted political cynicism over the individualist positions represented
by the other two. But as Müller clearly stated in an interview, the play presents 'three false attitudes to reality, to history': Odysseus' position is thus just as false as the others'.
In what then does this falsity consist? One answer is to be
found in Odysseus' speech to Philoctetes as he begs him
for his life:

> Now I would set you free from this exile
> And grant you a long-deserved eternal fame.
> By killing me you kill three thousand men
> And those three thousand dead will Troy preserve
> And Troy preserved will mean our cities' doom.
> You think you set your foot upon my neck
> It is the very earth that holds you up
> If I should never see my home again
> You will not either, I am your native land
> Its fields and pastures live and die with me.

The reasons Odysseus offers Philoctetes are all based
on calculations of rational self-interest: an opportunity for
'eternal fame' and to defeat the threat posed by the Trojans
and return home. None of them address the existential
question of whether it is actually worth going on living in

the kind of society that treats its members as it has treated Philoctetes. To do this, Odysseus would have to offer him some purpose or meaning for his years of suffering beyond that of immediate political expediency, and it is precisely this that he cannot do—Odysseus' pragmatism is of a kind that has lost sight of its own purpose and become a position of pure manipulation. He can offer Philoctetes no reason to return with him beyond mere physical survival and the prospect of being used again in another tactical game. For Philoctetes, weary of suffering, this is not reason enough.

Philoctetes has been commonly interpreted as an allegory of the rehabilitation of Communist Party members who were imprisoned or persecuted under Stalin. Following Khrushchev's secret speech of 1956, the crimes committed under Stalin began slowly to be recognized. But it was recognition of a limited kind—while some injustices were acknowledged, the deeper reasons behind them, such as the crushing of Party democracy and the betrayal of revolutionary political aims, never were. In the figures of Odysseus and Philoctetes, Müller presents the allegory of a Stalinist Party official trying to entice one of his victims back into participating in a society that remains committed to the very politics of cynical pragmatism that led to his persecution. So one 'correct' attitude to history that his audience is to derive from the three 'false' ones is that, without a revival of genuinely radical politics, society will never be able to unite around the tasks facing it.

The next play, *The Horatian*, is both a development and expansion on this theme. Its subject is also taken from the classical past, this time Livy's history of early Rome. The two warring city states, Rome and Alba, find themselves facing the common threat of a powerful Etruscan army. To preserve their strength against this common enemy, they decide that a representative from each side should resolve their differences in single combat. Rome chooses a Horatian, Alba a Curiatian; the two men fight, and the Curiatian is wounded. He begs for mercy, reminding the Horatian that he is betrothed to his sister; but the Horatian replies, 'my bride is Rome', and kills his opponent. Upon his victorious return home he is enraged to find his grieving sister refusing to embrace him; and he kills her as well. At this point, the cheering of the crowds 'falls silent', as the Roman people look on in horror at what he has done. The rest of the play is concerned with their deliberations over what to do with this 'victor-murderer' who has killed 'once for Rome and once not for Rome'.

The essence of these deliberations is to determine whether he should be 'honoured as a victor or punished as a murderer'. In the course of them, several solutions are proposed. One is that his victory and crime cancel each other out; another is that both should be simply forgotten in the public interest. But these are rejected in favour of the conclusion that neither act can be forgotten, and both must be fully recognized. Thus the Horatian must be judged *both* victor and murderer, and be *both* honoured and punished. Accordingly, he is first crowned with laurels, and the entire Roman people kneel before him. He then has the laurels torn from his brows and is beheaded. The same procedure is used again in the treatment of his corpse: his 'reassembled' body is solemnly borne aloft on his comrades' shoulders, before being thrown to the dogs in an act of desecration. Discussion then turns to how the Horatian is to be remembered by posterity, and the conclusion mirrors the judgement passed upon him—he is to be remembered as both a victor and a murderer, and those who acknowledge the one fact and not the other are to be reviled. This, it becomes clear, is not merely a measure aimed at preserving justice and social harmony but language itself, and the capacity language offers for making sense of the world:

> For our words must remain pure. For
> A sword can be broken and a man
> Can also be broken, but words
> Fall irrevocably into the workings of the world
> Leaving things knowable or unknowable.
> And lethal to us is what we cannot know.

In contrast to *Philoctetes*, *The Horatian* shifts the role of judge of the events from the audience to the performers themselves—it is this that lies behind its combination of all speaking parts into a single verse block, whose lines can be distributed at the players' own discretion. Müller later made clear that this change was inspired by contemporary events:

> My earlier plan provided for an open end: the
> audience as judge. At the end of 1968 the freedom
> of choice no longer seemed to me to be a given
> . . . the terribly simple (naïve) solution seemed
> realistic.

The date of the play is crucial to its allegory. For 1968 was the year of the Soviet invasion of Czechoslovakia and the crushing of its brief period of reform Communism known as the 'Prague Spring'. Rome and Alba are thus now revealed as the two Communist states, Soviet and Czech, while the Etruscans, their common enemy, are the Western powers confronting them. It is notable that Müller's treatment of the allegory does not, as one might expect it would, clearly come down on the side of the reformists against the hardliners. Rather, it proposes a way for both sides to successfully resolve their differences that does proper justice to the events of the past. The figure of the Horatian, and the subject of the two sides' dispute, is of course Stalin himself—or perhaps more accurately, the 'Stalinized' parties and politics that were his legacy. Coming to terms with that legacy means grasping it in its full contradictory nature as one of both victory and murder—victory over Nazi Germany, and the murder of many thousands of innocent people. At the same time, it also requires the recognition that this resolution will never be complete: there will always be a 'remainder . . . that cannot be unmade', an irreducible residue of loss and suffering that cannot be made amends for or overcome, but only spoken of, as part of the 'impure truth'.

While *The Horatian* takes a theme from *Philoctetes* and develops and expands it, *Mauser* goes on to do the same with *The Horatian*, and thereby directly approaches the series' basic problematic, that of revolutionary violence itself. In *Mauser*, Müller abandons the classical settings of the earlier two plays for a twentieth-century one. But for all this it remains an allegory, albeit a more complex and ambiguous one than the earlier works. Its historical subject, as Müller informs us in his note, is taken from the Soviet writer Mikhail Sholokhov's novel *And Quiet Flows the Don*, and deals with a Party activist caught up in the violent events of the Red Terror that followed the Bolshevik seizure of power in 1917. Its literary subject, however, is the *Lehrstücke* themselves; of all the plays in the series, it offers the most self-conscious reflection on the form itself, its text reading like a bricolage of quotations from and allusions to Brecht's works. The most important of these is the latter's famous, not to say notorious, *Lehrstück* from 1930, *The Measures Taken*.

The Measures Taken takes the form of a dialogue between three Communist Party activists and a Control Chorus, representing the central Party authorities. The Activists have just returned from a mission to China, where their task has been to spread revolutionary propaganda among the workers. Their mission, they report, was successful, but in order to ensure its success they were forced to kill one of their own members. They request that the Chorus hear their account of it, and give its judgement on this decision.

The activists tell their story by performing it, each of them assuming a different part. In China, they explain, they met a young sympathizer—the Young Comrade—who offered to help them in their work. The Activists gave him a series of tasks to perform—spreading propaganda, arming the workers, organizing for an uprising—at which he successively failed. In each case, his failure was caused by an excess of 'humanity': the Young Comrade put his feelings of sympathy for the workers and loathing for their oppressors before rational reflection and tactical consideration. On each occasion, his comrades discussed with him where he went wrong and encouraged him to do better the next time. His final error, however, proved catastrophic: he organized a premature revolt of workers which was brutally suppressed by the authorities. Forced to flee, the activists decided that their only way to evade capture and save the mission was to kill the Young Comrade, whose identity had become known, and destroy his body. They proposed this to him and, after considering the alternatives, he consented. The Activists shot him and threw his body into the chalk pit, thereby preserving the secrecy of their mission. The Party committee, having heard their account, approves their action.

The controversy around *The Measures Taken* rapidly ensured it became the most famous of Brecht's *Lehrstücke*. While extremely popular at the time of staging, it was also widely denounced as an apologia for the ruthless political methods employed by Communist parties. Even those parties themselves treated it with circumspection, wary of the 'bad reputation' it might give their cause. As a result, the play remained unstaged for years after its initial performance, with Brecht himself refusing almost all requests for a revival. It is with this controversial text that Müller's play engages.

Mauser also takes the form of a dialogue between an individual activist, in this case known only as A, and a Chorus; but in it the task facing the two is quite different. They are not preparing the way for a revolutionary uprising but defending a revolutionary government that has come to power. Their mission is no longer the vanguard one of agitational and propaganda work among the masses but the 'struggle in the rear': the suppression and extermination of the new government's political enemies.

It is a struggle that has simultaneously grown more violent and more abstract than the one in Brecht's play. *Mauser* sets aside all the tactical questions explored in *The Measures Taken* to concentrate on the single issue of political murder. In contrast to the variety and complexity of the tasks the Young Comrade is required to perform, A's have shrunk to the grotesquely repetitive one of endless killing; the process of learning and teaching is here reduced to the monstrous 'lesson . . . of the bullet'. The revolutionary tasks aimed at overcoming alienation and dehumanization have themselves become supremely alienating and dehumanizing, while the choices left open to A have narrowed to the single one of killing or not killing, in circumstances where, as the Chorus reminds him, his task 'must be / Performed by someone else if not by you'. Indeed, refusing the task barely seems an option at all—the stakes are already too high, the moral pressure too overwhelming. At the same time, this narrowing of the scope for action has been accompanied by a vast expansion in the scope for error. In *The Measures Taken*, the Young Comrade commits three mistakes before his final, fatal one; A, by contrast, is killed for just one—if mistake it can be called at all. The change in the nature of the revolutionary tasks demanded by the situation also changes the nature of the error A commits. While the Young Comrade fails through an excess of humanity, a placing of empathy before rational calculation, A's failure might be called an excess of inhumanity, an instance of uncontrollable and violent psychic breakdown, which he is able to anticipate but not avoid.

The nature of the debate between the protagonist and Chorus has also changed. In *Mauser*'s circumstances of generalized atrocity, A and the Chorus discuss both the practical issues of killing and dying and the abstract question of what it means to be human, in a debate that interweaves the two. The paradox of the Revolution is that it is made in the name of a humanity that does not yet exist, a humanity that the very making of the Revolution is supposed to bring into being. A's first appeal against his sentence of death is ultimately that of his own fallibility, explained in terms of his humanity: 'I've made a mistake . . . I'm human'. But when asked to define what it means to be human, he can only come up with his own desire to live ('I don't want to die'). Against this claim, the Chorus insists that no definition can be given until the preconditions for the actual existence of humanity have been met. And they will not be met unless the Revolution is successful:

> For not until the Revolution's won
> In Vitebsk as in cities everywhere
> Shall we know what a human being is.

A appears to be able to accept this argument in theory, but its practical implications are too much for him. The ruthless sacrifices it demands—first of his moral scruples, then of his life itself—seem impossible to make in the absence of the guarantee that they will not be made in vain. And yet, as the Chorus insists, it is precisely in the absence of this guarantee that he must act. Its reply to this vital question, the one that might sustain him in his work, is unequivocal, and hardly reassuring:

A

When the Revolution's won will killing stop.
And will it win. How much longer still.

CHORUS

We know what you know, you know what we know.

The Chorus, representing the revolutionary collective, knows no more than A, and can offer him no moral assurances for what it requires him to do. What hope there is, it claims, will only arise through (collective) praxis: it is by intervening in the situation that the truth of it will be created.

Thus A is caught between the human being as it actually exists, as a suffering, mortal being, and the human being as it might be, brought into existence by the violence of history. His position—the position of the revolutionary—is one of radical exclusion from both, of unbearable exile. Like the Young Comrade in *The Measures Taken*, it is precisely the suspension of empathy that A cannot endure; but unlike him, A is able only to ignore his feelings of 'humanity' at the cost of transforming them into their opposite, an excess of 'inhumanity'. Empathy turns into ecstatic rage.

A (CHORUS)

I take beneath my heels what I have killed
And dance on it to pound its face to pulp
For I am not content to kill what must
Die if the Revolution is to win
And killing end, but it must disappear
From the earth's face forever, leaving behind
A new world for the generations to come.

It should be noted that the mistake that condemns A is not, as with the Young Comrade or his predecessor B, a substantive disobeying of orders: in the play, A only ever kills those he has been ordered to kill. The difference consists rather in the *manner* in which he kills them, for it is this that reveals his inability to draw the distinction between 'human beings'—which do no yet exist—and 'enemies', which are only too real. His mistake consists not in the individuals, but in the *subjects* he kills: A's crime is to kill prisoners *as if* they were people (that is to say, with an irrational excess of violence), rather than *as if* they were enemies (that is to say, with proportionate, rational violence). The distinction may seem abstract, but for the Party it is crucial. An inability to distinguish between human being and enemy makes A himself an enemy: by it he excludes himself from the revolutionary collective, and from the future society that collective is trying to create. This, according to the Chorus, is why he has to die:

> We heard him howl and saw what he had done
> Without our orders and that he would not stop
> Screaming with the human voice of one
> Who preys on human beings. Then we knew
> That his work had used him up and that his time
> Was over and we led him off as we
> Would any enemy of the Revolution
> And not like any, but his own enemy too

The Chorus requires of A that he agree to his death *without* the certainty of its ultimately serving some higher purpose. All he can confidently consider his own is his fear. While A eventually consents to die, it remains ambiguous how willingly he does so; he remains a figure of division to the end.

Like Brecht's play before it, Müller's quickly became the subject of controversy, finding itself attacked, although for very different reasons, in both east and west. The East German authorities lost no time in condemning it as counter-revolutionary, and *Mauser* became the only one of Müller's plays to be officially banned in his own country. By contrast, several West German critics saw in it a justification for revolutionary violence in general and Stalin's crimes in particular.

Both interpretations fundamentally misunderstand the play. *Mauser* is neither a condemnation nor a glorification of revolutionary violence but a presentation of the kind of arguments that would be needed to justify it. And whether one agrees with them or not, it is important to understand that these arguments are emphatically *not* Stalinist. For the Chorus' repeated insistence on its own historical ignorance is a position that Stalinist ideology would never have tolerated. As Slavoj Žižek, among others, has pointed out, the Stalinist justification for acts of political violence was always made from a position of supposedly privileged knowledge, one that offered exclusive insight into the 'objective meaning' of their own and others' actions. In the Stalinist view, the Party is able to see the present with a kind of historical hindsight, as if it occupied some notional point outside history that revealed to it contemporary events in their definitive significance. This fantasy of access to an absolute truth was the ultimate justification for all its many acts of political murder.

This, however, is the opposite of the Chorus' argument in *Mauser*. Instead of offering certainties, it insists it has no privileged view of things; instead of defining the humanity in whose name the Revolution is being made, it insists that it cannot be known. This is a far more uncompromising position than the Stalinist one, for it requires that one accept the full moral consequences of one's actions in circumstances where one cannot know what those consequences will be. Indeed, if anyone's position could be described as Stalinist in *Mauser*, it is that of A himself, who demands to know 'here and now' what a human being is, when the Revolution will eventually triumph, and who finally begs for reassurance that his death, and the deaths of those he has killed, will not have been in vain.

It is precisely these demands, which Stalinism indulged and exploited, that a genuinely revolutionary politics must refuse. The point is not that Stalinism was too severe, but rather that, in this crucial respect, *it was not severe enough*, and that its crimes were effectively the consequence of this lack of severity. By indulging these demands, it laid open the way for the corruption of its revolutionary subjects and its own degeneration into another ideology of oppression. For the methods of the Revolution cannot be justified in terms of its inevitable triumph or the 'objective guilt' of its enemies: to do so is to surrender responsibility for one's actions, and thereby betray the possibility of genuine human freedom that the Revolution sought to establish. We might recall at this point the manner in which the *Lehrstück* is supposed to be performed: the argument it advances is not supposed to be passively accepted by an audience but analyzed and debated by those performing it. This does not preclude them rejecting the Chorus' arguments or proposing answers to the questions that it considers unanswerable. But it is at this point too, the present in which it is performed, that the question of its allegory poses itself most relevantly. *Mauser* clearly alludes to the Stalinist purges of the 1930s, that paroxysm of bloodletting that destroyed for good the revolutionary hopes of October. It is not, however, itself an allegory of those events. Rather, it might be seen as a utopian or perhaps counter-factual allegory—an allegory of events that did not happen but might have. For in it, it is the revolutionary collective that triumphs, and the Stalinist reactionaries that are led to the wall.

Uwe Schütte,
2000

PHILOCTETES

Prologue

(*The actor playing Philoctetes appears in a clown mask.*)
Ladies and gentlemen, the play you'll shortly see
Moves from the present to Antiquity
When men in mortal fear of others went
And human life in brutal struggle spent.
Let us make clear right now: we do not preach
We have no lessons for our times to teach
Nor homilies on how men ought to live.
If you don't like that, here's your chance to leave.
(*The doors of the auditorium open.*)
You have been warned.
(*The doors close. The clown removes his mask: beneath it is a
    skull.*)
                    Few of you will find
Amusing what our players have in mind.

Coast. Odysseus. Neoptolemos.

ODYSSEUS.
This is the place, Lemnos. It was here
That I marooned Philoctetes of Melos
Who, wounded in our service, had become
Unserviceable once his wound began
To stink and ooze with pus, and when his howls
Cut short our sleep and rang unseemly through
The silence that the sacrifice demands.
His dwelling is that hill, or at least
I hope it to be so, and not his grave;
A hole washed by the water from the rock
In labour measureless, when fish still swam
What we dry-footed tread. Before it flows a spring.
If in the last ten years it has not dried.
Find me his dwelling. Then hear my plan
And all that in it falls to you.

NEOPTOLEMOS.
                                This mission
Takes me no distance.

ODYSSEUS.
                        Empty?

NEOPTOLEMOS.
                              A bed of leaves.
A drinking bowl carved from unseasoned wood.
Flints. Rags hung up to dry in the wind
Stained black with blood.

ODYSSEUS.
                                        Still bleeding then.
He can't walk far with his old injury.
He's seeking food or herbs to ease the pain.
Let him not take us unawares for he
Would sooner kill me than any man alive.

NEOPTOLEMOS.
Quite rightly. You swung the axe that cut him off.

ODYSSEUS.
Now you must be the net that draws him back.

NEOPTOLEMOS.
All sense slips through your words. What do you want?

ODYSSEUS.
That in our cause you do not spare yourself.

NEOPTOLEMOS.
I do not live my life just to preserve it.

ODYSSEUS.
Something I mean worth more to you than life.
Deceive him into giving up his bow
Such words from me would be returned with darts
But you were never party to his fate
He never saw your face among our ships
Cleaving your tongue, you'll catch him easily
Who once disarmed is easily brought to ship.

NEOPTOLEMOS.
I'm here to help our cause, and not to lie.

ODYSSEUS.
And yet that cause needs someone here who'll lie.

NEOPTOLEMOS.
The truth might help us more.

ODYSSEUS.
                                        Not ours with him.

NEOPTOLEMOS.
What can a cripple do against two men?

ODYSSEUS.
Too much, so long he has his bow with him.

NEOPTOLEMOS.
Then we will meet his arrows with our own.

ODYSSEUS.
Who'll follow a dead general into battle?

NEOPTOLEMOS.
Perhaps the arrows drawn upon our bows
Will keep his in his quiver.

ODYSSEUS.
                                        To him our deaths
Are dearer than his life. And there's no man living
On Lemnos who isn't needed now at Troy.

NEOPTOLEMOS (*throws down his spear*).
I could drag him bare-handed to the ship.

ODYSSEUS (*picks up the spear*).
Keep your daring for later. Here I need you wise
A dead man's cunning is no use to me.
You'd best learn that from me than from his bow.
If you go now, you won't be coming back.

NEOPTOLEMOS.
Let me. You can stay and worry here.

ODYSSEUS.
Take another step and I will nail
You to this island with your father's spear.
And Hercules won't help you, as he did
The immortals' thief, whom they bound to the rock
With those rapacious birds for company.
Your flesh is not the kind that will grow back
The vultures here will pick it from these stones.

NEOPTOLEMOS.
Much bravery you show to one unarmed.

ODYSSEUS.
I show you what an unarmed man can do.

NEOPTOLEMOS.
With my spear. And not for the first time now
I see my own possessions in those hands
So skilled in theft, especially from me
You desecrate the arms my father bore
When hands he had to use them, the bronze blade
Battered and hacked, the many-scarred hide.
Return to me just one spear that is mine
And I'll show you what I can do with it.

ODYSSEUS.
Show me some other time, some other place.
I too have seen your spear stained red with blood
And never doubted of your skill in battle.
But you and I still need each other living.
By accident of birth my spear commands
A thousand others, a thousand that are yours
And yet another thousand spears are saved
Or lost with it, if you refuse this task.
For this I brought you from your home to Troy

From Skyros, before you had tasted life
After your father's too untimely death
When his men had quit the battle, and sat upon
His hill, swigging his wine and portioning out
His wives among themselves, the two rewards
Denied them in the struggle to amass
The honour and the plunder of their lord.
Who spitted Hector on his spear for him?
We needed you to drive them back to war
As we need him for his loyal troops
Not for your arm, still untried in battle
Not for his arm, small use to use alone
But because men more willingly will risk their lives
Driven by bootheels shod in native leather.
It isn't for myself I bear your arms
But in the battle for your father's body
When men died to save a corpse, my company
Bled more than any other, and their scars burned.
And burn no longer, now they see me wear
Your father's arms as payment for their wounds.
Should I return to Ilium without him
His warriors would turn their backs on us
And on our war. The Trojans wash themselves
White with our blood, and with our flesh they gorge
Their country's vultures. That you have no great skill
In lying and stealing, that I know full well.
But sweet, Achilles' son, is victory.
Therefore but for a single day, no more,
Blacken your tongue, the rest of your life live
In virtue, for as long as it may last.
Refuse, and darkness waits to claim us all.

NEOPTOLEMOS.
No healthy plant can grow from blighted ground.

ODYSSEUS.
The ground is one thing, the tree is quite another.

NEOPTOLEMOS.
In storms a tree is tested by its roots.

ODYSSEUS.
But not a forest.

NEOPTOLEMOS.
Which is consumed by fire.

ODYSSEUS.
Or floods, which break up all the ground beneath.
Each force repels the other, what comes must go
We can discuss this further on Troy's ruins.

NEOPTOLEMOS.
I wish I had no ears for what you say.
Tell me the lies that I must tell to him.

ODYSSEUS.
Your spear. You need not lie in every thing.
Be who you are, son of Achilles, the first sword
At Troy, until the ravisher's bow shot
The mortal dart into his too bold flesh.
Then lie: say you are bound for home, your sails
Filled with hate for us, and me especially.
We summoned you to glory and to Troy
While still your father's ashes warmed their urn
Because his soldiers' grief for him too long
Had stalled our many wearied years of siege;
You came, but most dishonourably we denied
Your rightful claim to your inheritance
Your much-lamented father's sword and spear;
And I it was deceived you, speaking lies,
And I it was that stole your legacy.

NEOPTOLEMOS.
Speak more like this, you won't see Troy again.

ODYSSEUS.
Open your veins, and slake the bloodlust there
That nourished you first at your mother's breast
Or with the butt of this your father's spear
I'll thrash you back into our covenant.

NEOPTOLEMOS.
So long as Troy still stands, my duty binds
My hatred to the foe, only his defeat
Will let me bathe my spear in other blood.
Don't hasten that day now with reckless words.

ODYSSEUS.
Save your bile for your task. Heap so much filth
Upon my name as might content your heart
It cannot hurt me if it helps our cause
Cloud his eye to your true purpose so that he
Will guilelessly give up his lethal bow
Into your hands, in earnest certitude
They yearn as much as his to spill my blood.
I chose you because you do not need to lie
Your lies will be convincing for their truth
With them I'll use one foe to catch another.
If shame should flood your face he'll think it's rage
Which it may be, for you yourself won't tell
What swifter drives the blood into your head
Shame that you lie, or rage because you don't
The more your face is blackened by your lies
The sweeter will your truths sound to his ears.

NEOPTOLEMOS.
Then you'll need someone else to serve your cause.

ODYSSEUS.
Do you think you're the first to desecrate
Your principles? It is our common fate.
Your father shamed himself when he disguised

Himself in women's clothes, and it was I
Unmasked him when I donned a peddler's guise
And to the palace women hawked my wares
When he disdained the spindles for the blades
He proved himself, what none had seen, a man.
The princes snared me for their war with Troy
In just this way: when I madness feigned
And sowed the earth with salt, walking behind
A team of oxen whom I called my lords
And seeming not to know my dearest friends
They tore from my wife's breast my infant son
And threw him before the plough. I scarce had time
To rein the harnessed beasts before their hooves
Manured with his most precious blood the earth
Which I to save myself had sowed with salt.
And so they judged me to be sound of mind
But I was made to honour our alliance.
Enough of this. How would you have me? Kneeling?
(*Kneels.*)

NEOPTOLEMOS.
How sweet it would be to be a Trojan now.
How practised is your knee to kiss the earth
This is the way you came before my father
Genuflecting, grovelling to assuage
His fury that your perfidy had stirred
In pilfering his fame, and tricking out
Yourselves in glory that was rightly his.

ODYSSEUS.
It irked him that we made him share the spoils
Your father was much wiser than his son.
He knew our downcast eyes searched in the dust
For rocks: and that if he succumbed to rage
We'd both be dead, and all his booty lost.
If I kneel now, then it is for your life.

(*Stands up.*)
Here comes your catch. His tread uneven still.
Don't look at me. Unless you want to die
Before you've slaked your craving for my blood.

NEOPTOLEMOS.
More like a beast than man he seems to me
A cloud of vultures swarms about his head.

ODYSSEUS.
Beware his bow, as long as he still has it.
But more than that, beware of his despair
Til he in chains or free has followed us
To Troy, where Asclepios will cure his foot
So he can cure us of that greater wound
From which too long two peoples' blood has flowed
And stinking save us from the stench of battle.
Blinding yourself to it, you'll heal his wound
Deafening yourself to them, you'll still his cries
The matter now rests in your hands alone
And I can only beg the cunning god
To grant you but a little cunning more.
Athena give you victory, whom Zeus
Hewed from his head, to bring a goddess forth.
(*Exit. Enter Philoctetes.*)

PHILOCTETES.
What living thing befouls my lifeless shore?
What beast that walks erect as once did I
On other soil when still my legs were whole?
What are you, two-legs? Human, beast or Greek?
And if the latter, reckon to be no more.
(*Neoptolemos runs off.*)
Had you a thousand legs with which to flee
My darts fly faster.
(*Neoptolemos stops.*)
                    Throw away your sword.

(*Neoptolemos does so.*)
In what tongue was it, dog, you learned to lie
Which was the bitch that whelped you in this world
What good or evil tempest drove your ship
Upon my shore, that every boat has spurned
Since I in vain have scanned the sea for sails
My vision failing, trailed by a cheering cloud
Of carrion birds that shroud the glaring sky
In patient expectation of my ruin
Or else the wreckage of a stricken ship
To save me from the bellies of the fish.
You're dressed in Grecian clothes, as once was I.
And Grecian dress may well beclothe a Greek.
Or is it that you've killed a Greek, my friend?
For friend I'll call you if a Greek has died
By your hand, and shall never ask the cause:
He was a Greek, you need no other grounds.
Should you send me to dwell among the shades
Your motives need no pleading: I'm a Greek.
But I'll perform the killer if it prove
That you are what your clothes suggest, a Greek.
For Greeks it was that left me here upon
This salt-rimed rock, when wounded in their cause
I proved no longer serviceable to them
And Greeks it was who watched and did not help.
These rags are all that's left of them, and you
Can see how much remains now of the Greek:
A corpse that feeds itself from its own grave.
That grave has room for more than just its corpse.
Tell me, before my arrow draws from you
Your last breath in reply, are you a Greek?
Your silence says you are and strings the bow
Then die and feed the vultures that feed me
Offering them a foretaste of my flesh.

NEOPTOLEMOS.
These are foul words to welcome your first guest
And foul the dish that you have offered me
Who after such long voyage hoped to find
A bed more ample than a vulture's belly.
Had I known it was customary here
To greet your guests with arrows and to feed
Their flesh to vultures, I would have left my host
Unseen and with all haste have turned my prow
To the hospitable ocean once again
And left you to your isle, and it to you.

PHILOCTETES.
So sweet to me this sound. So long unheard
This tongue in which I uttered my first word
In which I drove a thousand oarsmen on
And steered a thousand warriors to war.
And loathed as long as unheard. And longer still.
For years I heard it only from my lips
When pain from my clenched teeth tore human cries
Which these indifferent cliffs all multiplied
And sent them back rebounding to my ear.
My ear so yearns to hear another voice.
Then live, because you have a voice to utter.
And speak. Tell me the worst, tell me that
My enemies thrive. Tell me what you will.
And lie. For far too long I've heard no lies.
Where is your ship? Where are you from? And where
Upon what business do you go? Have you any?
Do you know who stands before you, strange to himself
One-legged, the other suppurating flesh?
I never saw your face among my foes
And beardless, you've not borne your arms so long
As I have borne this blackened stinking limb
And yet I know their tongues are apt enough
To blacken the very shadow that I cast

Even among the unborn and the dead.
Tell me what lies they told you to tell here
To what injustice have you lent your hand
Have I survived too long to suit my killers
Are you their bloodhound, set on a bloody trail
To finish off their much-tormented quarry
Before it tears the gullets from their dogs?
I'll leave you breath enough to speak the truth.
Live three words longer. Speak.

NEOPTOLEMOS.
I don't know who you are nor your misfortune.
Your bow would feed these vultures innocent blood.

PHILOCTETES.
Silence, Greek, or I'll tear out your voice.
Maybe you don't know where the storm has brought you.
To know this island is to know of me.
For our two names are uttered in one breath
And every stone has breath enough to cry
That I am both their bondsman and their lord
Shackled to them by these encircling tides
That fetter us in endless solitude
I, Philoctetes, and Lemnos my domain.

NEOPTOLEMOS.
I have heard speak of Lemnos, not of you.
And we from Skyros are not wont to lie.

PHILOCTETES.
Yet it might be some lying cattle thief
From Ithaca, who stole your father's herd
Quitted his theft upon the marriage bed
By servicing your mother with his seed
And then on Skyros from this liar's seed
There grew another: you. Don't touch that spear.
Be what you are, a liar, killer, thief

You have a ship, I need no more from you
A place among your oarsmen, or beneath.
Do you still have a ship? Then take my feet
From off this alien soil, and from my sight
The shadows of my vultures. Or has the storm
Shattered your hull, and must I henceforth share
My birds with you, until that meagre fare
Is by our twofold hunger all consumed
And we unburied moulder in the sun.

NEOPTOLEMOS.
Neoptolemos I am, Achilles' son.
Homewards I sail to Skyros, leaving Troy
Behind, tasked to restore an injured honour.
Spare your arrows for my enemy, for yours
He is too, Ithaca's crowned cur.

PHILOCTETES.
The fellowship of fools welcomes you.
Did you perform a service to the Greeks?
How right they were to punish you for it.
For only could a Greek be such a fool
As raise his hand to help another Greek.
Tell me of other things, tell me these past years
How long the war for Priam's city raged
And who of friend or foe lies buried there:
For I sailed out to Troy with the first fleet
And lost the fight before the first encounter
Here, where there's no tree to mark the years
And where the sun rolls ever the same course
And ever the same phases turns the moon
Beneath the wandering of the farthest stars
On its dark orbit, unmoving to the eye.
A thousand nights sufficed to sicken me
Of its decline and rise. Tell me how long
Have I been my own enemy in my war.

He harrowed me with arms more terrible
Than the armoured Trojan legions ever bore
And ground me in the dust beneath his foot
Yet pain was not the worst that I endured.
The horror was my enemy had no face.
I craved to see myself in my own eyes
Or nail with arrows to the sun the wind
That stirs with waves the mirror of the sea.
I hoped to see my face in vultures' eyes
But only arrows bring them in my reach
And blind their gaze to mine and mine to theirs.
Then for no longer than a fleeting instant
Could I still hope to see my face again
But for that instant I'd have gladly died
And gladly slowly, to see myself so long.
I'd be the last man I'd see alive
Before I fed the hunger of my guests.
And what remained, those unassuming bones
Would with the seasons ever lighter grow
Til scattered by the winds. Then nothing more.
You have two eyes, here, let me see my face.
I see your eyes have robbed me of my face.
Then cover up eyes, Greek, for they lie.
Hide them before I tear my image from
Your eyes with my own nails. Or else my gaze
Is lying and I myself am nothing but
A vacant memory of one who's dead.
You stop your breath when you come close to me
Which tells me that my stench is real enough.
Tell me how many died and how much time
Has passed since I, enfevered by my wound,
Unseen, unheard, my cries lost to the wind,
Gazed as the fleet shrank over the horizon
Irrevocable, its dying plash of oars
Already by another sound usurped
The rustle of the beating wings that plough

Furrows invisible in the pathless sky.
You needn't rush to answer. Be they ten
Or a hundred years, no god can turn them back
No tears can turn this dust back into flesh.
Nor is there anyone left dear to me.
My eyes have tears now only for a corpse
A thing of flesh, three-headed and six-tongued
That I'd be most reluctant to see dead,
Since what is dead cannot be killed again
Not twice and not a thousand times and not
His whole life long and not my whole life long.

NEOPTOLEMOS.
The city's still untaken, and the war
Now ten years old. The generals all live
Despised by both of us. The Ithacan
My enemy and yours, still lives as well.
Achilles is by Paris' arrow slain
And Ajax too, by his own hand and sword
Who bore Achilles' body from the fray.
The generals had set the hero's arms
As bounty for the rescue of his body:
Shield, sword and spear, my rightful legacy
In hope that in the struggle for his corpse
They might enlist the dead man in their cause
And with him breach a hole in Troy's redoubt.
Beneath Troy's walls his body lay, abused
With stones and spittle from a shrieking crowd
Of frenzied women widowed by his sword.
Ajax bore him away, and paid the price
In blood, but then Odysseus, with hand unscathed
Plucked the very bounty of his wounds
And claimed as it his own. The generals connived
And granted for the favours of a slave
What wasn't theirs to give nor his to take.
Then when Ajax defrauded decried the fraud

And showed in empty hands the bloody cost
Before the villains' tents, the robber scorned
His pleas and swindled him of his own right.
Ajax then to quench his rage drank wine
And blind with drinking fell that night upon
The herds, and killed the cattle they had stole
Thinking in his madness they were Greeks.
At dawn he saw himself as they saw him
Steeped in the blood of beasts, raw strips of flesh
Clenched in his hands, and craved another blood.
Then to the sea he ran with crimson sword
Amid the laughter of the opposing hosts
And bathed his body and the blade of blood
Then firmly set its hilt into the earth
And ran the long route down it into night
Watering the alien shore with his own blood.
All this is not the least of what occurred
While I on Skyros still was riding nags.
In hope they could use me to fill their ranks
The generals sent the Ithacan to my home.
He came to me with treaties and sweet words
Hiding from me my father's sword and spear
The rightful legacy that he had stolen
Til I was in his net, and Troy's walls
Before my eyes, and at my back the sea
Knowing that if I raised arms in my cause
Before we'd ground its ramparts into dust
Unconquered Troy would ravage all our lands.
And yet I found I could not choke my heart
I could not march to battle with the man
Who'd torn the sword and shield from his chest
The very dust that had engendered me
When it was living flesh. And so I quit the war
In hope the foe would spare my foe for me.

PHILOCTETES.
Our hatred has a common enemy
And what we both once loved manures the earth.
You have a ship, let's hasten to the shore
Take me to Melos. Let each of us then wait
Upon our coasts, scanning the sea each day
For his return, and pray the winds and tides
Carry him safely to our joint embrace.
(*Howls.*)
You have a sword, boy, sever off this foot.
The pain returns, the many-taloned bird
Circles and wheels, rends through the putrid flesh
The insomniac guest gets out of bed again
To entertain the host with his own howls.
O man, you have a sword, so cut it off.
Who was it turned your living heart to stone.
Or give the blade here, while the pain allows
Me to take a sword and hack it off.

NEOPTOLEMOS.
Here, take my shoulder, and give me the bow
Until your leg can bear your weight again.
Your arrows too, so they won't pierce your side
When you are doubled over by the pain.

PHILOCTETES.
Don't touch my bow, Greek. Til I can stand again
Tell me of Melos, fairest of our isles.
How long is it since I beheld the woods
From which we cut our swift and sombre ships.
How long have I cursed him who, shod with ships
First wandered the sea's pathways to become
The author of my exile and return
For which I'd have him ever more revered.
How long have I been my own man and wife
Deprived of the fair sex, that other wound

And left no exit from my body's chains
But watching seabirds mate upon the surf
Of these salt tides, whose waves perpetual
Caress this rust-red rock, my stony bed.
Take me to Melos, help my foot to bear
What it can't carry where I yearn to go.
And lend me your hand to take this bow of mine
Til I can bear it in my hand again.
It lent my hunger wings, and made the sky
My hunting ground, put clouds within my grasp.
I never gave it any one til now
Since Heracles first pressed it in my hand
In payment for the service rendered him
Which I, his son refusing, did perform
When he from Nessus' shirt in torment burned:
I lit the pyre that he had built himself
And pulled the flaming curtain down upon
The world he could no longer bear to see:
Earth, heaven, wife and children and his own
Mutinous roiling flesh. It has sustained
Most faithfully these many years of death
Til you arrived to raise me from the dead
To life, that knows no death before it ends.

NEOPTOLEMOS (*takes the bow*).
I wish I'd never Troy nor Lemnos seen
I wish I'd never set upon the path
That cleaves me from myself, that rends a wound
More terrible than any blade could carve
And time can never heal. The path I lead
Will soon enough be odious to you.

PHILOCTETES.
In many words you speak a single word.
Then does this stinking wound that exiled me
To be the vultures' ward offend you so

That you would leave me here a second time.
Return to me my bow and take your leave.
And spare your shipmates this unseemly freight
Your ears the discord of my tortured cries.
I shall forget I ever saw you here.
The shadow of a shadow crossed my isle
A mirage generated by the sun's
Noonday fornication on the rocks
Or else there spoke in human voice to me
The murmuring surf, or else a crow spewed up
The tongue of some dead Greek it had devoured
Before the walls of Troy, that jabbered still.
Time presses on us now. Give me the bow.
Ten years alone I've studied in the school
Which you have built for me. I need more time.
Now leave me to my vultures and myself.

NEOPTOLEMOS.
I can no longer lie. So hear the truth.
The city will not fall without your men
And they will only follow your command
I've come to fetch you back to Troy and bring
You from long torment to eternal fame
And much against my will I have deceived
One much betrayed, as I have been myself:
But saw my duty summoned me to lie.
Now, man of Lemnos, hear the truth entire
Grieved as I am to tell it: Odysseus
Waits on the beach, your enemy and mine
For there I did not lie: the day Troy falls
He dies by my hand, by ours, if you will.
To join us is to hasten both their ends
His and the war's, we need your arm with us
And voice that's worth a thousand arms. At Troy
Asclepios will heal your wounded foot
So come away, my hand burns with the bow
Which I from you too cunningly have got.

PHILOCTETES.
So was it shame that's blackening your face?
You needn't be ashamed of what you've done
I never saw a trap more neatly set
Nor with such pains a bait perform its task
Your master who first schooled you in deceit
Who taught you how to rob by robbing you
My-enemy-and-yours, will be most pleased.
My life, the bow that fed me, is in your hands
You want of nothing, your triumph's unalloyed
Now why not set your foot upon my neck
And teach the vanquished everything you've learned
From him that vanquished you, teach me how sweet
Oppression tastes, by sharing it with me
Teach me to lick up spit, to measure out
The earth by crawling on my chest to him
The general who set his foot upon
My neck when fever forced me to my knees.
Enemy's enemy, teach me your delights.
The joy of being beaten to the ground
The charms of being trampled underfoot
By one who ground my forebears in the dust.
You lying cur and filthy mouthed dog
Begotten by a satyr in a sty
Who in his swinish lust outplayed a boar
Whelped on a midden by a stablemaid
Discovered some by some vile and stinking king
Who drunk with wine bespewed the baby's head
That thus was crowned with filth and blessed with gall.
Take your face from out my sight, and take back
Into your mouth lies that I believed:
So sweet your voice rose from the cess of lies.
Spit your tongue into the sea to feed the fish
And teach them how to lie so artfully
Swallow up your breath so it won't foul
The air I breathe, choke on your own filth.

O sea. O sky. O ever-sightless stones
My foot chains me for ever to the earth
My folly casts me helpless to the world
An arrow's shot from here beneath the sun
There stands on two legs him I'd dearly wish
To trample underfoot, one who has returned
To cheat the vultures of a thing he had
Already left for them some time before.
Who to a new task curtly summons now
The servant he'd so long ago dismissed
And waits to see his bait bring back the catch,
That stinking flesh abandoned to the birds
Begrudged them now that same flesh is required
To feed some other vultures: for though it stinks
It acts as lure to one whose favoured odour
Will vanish once its catch has been devoured.
No carcass reeks as badly as your own
And you can never smell its stench yourself.
For all the kindness you have done me, do
One more, Achilles' son, if he you are
And did not lie to me in that as well:
And as you took my bow so take my breast
As quiver for your arrows, and to him
You stole it from return a little piece
Of what you stole, send that short shaft of iron
The distance from my sternum to my heart
Then pull the arrow from my lifeless breast
The silent witness of your infamy
And tell the Greeks your friends and first of all
The Ithacan, to whom you closer are
Than any since he stole your legacy
And if the war should spare you, tell your seed
That Philoctetes, the fool of Melos, died
Unmatched in folly, for he believed a Greek
Died a quiver for an arrow that had flown
From the bow that he'd commanded to be drawn

By the second greatest fool on Lemnos where
His folly exiled him, upon the isle
Where fools eat vultures, and the vultures fools.
And do not bury me in any grave
In foreign soil or native, lest my dust
Be mixed with yours by movement of the earth's
Blind hidden rocky streams, that rend the dead.
And do not burn my body on a pyre
Nor cast my ashes to the random winds
Lest they should one day mingle mine with yours.
And do not leave me out to feed the birds
Too many dead find shelter in their bellies.
Don't throw me to the fishes, lest it be
My flesh becomes a billet for your own.
And don't leave me to entertain the brine
That you may one day entertain yourself
Its endless discourse with your flesh and bones
Resolving them to brine and thus to me
For then as long as it remained at one
With itself, we'd be such to one another.
But bear me to the crater where the smoke
Drifts upwards from the sun that never sets
Nor rises, but is always to be felt
Burning beneath the feet, and drop me there
Where with this single foot I'll faster fall
Than with a thousand, through the thickening smoke
Into eternal fire. I've said my last. Dispatch.

NEOPTOLEMOS.
I wish the war had granted us reprieve
And with some other route afforded us
Escape than by our enemies' victory
Over our enemies: I would there might have been
Some other path to fame for you and me
Than this which I must now take to the beach
There to report the success of my deceit

And shame-faced render up the hostage caught
By lies to my own enemy and yours
With whom I'll bind and drag you to the ship
For if you duck the burden of the yoke
I must incline my neck to bear its weight
I'd sooner have your arrow in my chest
Than have to take your bow in these two hands.
(*Exits with bow.*)

PHILOCTETES.
Could I but turn myself into a dart
That kills and has a feel for what it kills.
Could I but sink the island with him on it
And savour his salt death as he was drowning
Before the ocean swallowed me itself.
My maker left me only half made up:
This hand, so skilled in arms, can't hope to fling
Myself a bow shot's distance, and this foot
That crushed so many men beneath its heels
Must tread a soil indifferent to its heel
The surface and the bowels of the earth
I need and can without them nothing be.
So listen, man of Lemnos, Philoctetes
My ear has heard your wailing long enough
Stop up your mouth from crying and set again
Your neck into the yoke, an aged hack
And midst Troy's slaughter learn to live again.
(*Stands.*)
You're needed. You're worth a trap to them again.
So run and take your place inside their net.
And though that scum may choke to hear your tread
Their duty stops their noses to your stench.
What's stopping you? Would you await another ship?
You have ten years, another will not come
It's only other chains will break these chains
Your enemy is now your only friend.

So swallow down the hatred that so long
Has better nourished you than vulture's flesh
And thank your enemy on bended knee
For giving it you. Store it in the nooks
And crannies of your body til the rage
Has grown so it devours all your hunger
The hope he'd die is what sustained your life
So wait a little more in greater hope.
And with a thousand arrows shield from death
The man for whom the thousand-first is meant.
You would have done the same if it had been
Another who stank and howled with poisoned flesh.
I was the wound, I the flesh that cried
After the singing topsails of the fleet
I who fed on vultures as years untold
Gnawed at my mind. I and I and I.
My hate was dearly bought, and mine alone.
My foot burns for the path that promises
To heal its brother, and return them whole
To human fellowship, the sickening weight
Of pain affords them wings, so forcefully
The baited line pulls on this rotting flesh.
So go, while there's still space beneath his heels
Take up the portion that's allotted you.
Live for his next kicking. Sweet it is
To live with those who suck each other's blood
Who succour one another with their fists
And spitting on each other offer alms.
So hurry to the filth that remedies
That heals the old wound with new injuries
And in the cess of battle cleans its sores.
(*Makes to leave.*)
Who comes?

Enter Odysseus, Neoptolemos.

ODYSSEUS.

One known to you, Philoctetes.

PHILOCTETES.
Who speaks with such familiar voice my name?

ODYSSEUS.
One who has your own voice not forgot
Since duty made him leave you to the birds.

PHILOCTETES.
One wounded in his service to that cause.

ODYSSEUS.
And with that wound no longer useful to it.

PHILOCTETES.
Philoctetes.

ODYSSEUS.

You.

PHILOCTETES.

Am I he? Who are you?

ODYSSEUS.
You know who. Odysseus. Don't play the fool.

PHILOCTETES.
Odysseus was a liar. If you are he
And say I'm Philoctetes, that can't be me.

ODYSSEUS.
It may be that Odysseus is such a liar
That he has made himself believe he was
Odysseus and thus by his lying makes
Himself himself no longer but another
And therefore not a liar, so if he calls
You Philoctetes then that is who you are.
Enough of this. Get up and come with us.

PHILOCTETES (*to Neoptolemos*).
Give me my bow, my friend, and one good bolt.

ODYSSEUS.
You can come freely or you can come bound
But we must leave together.
(*To Neoptolemos*)

Give me the rope.

PHILOCTETES.
Give me the bow. Cleanse the stain from off your name
Undo what you unwillingly have done.
A liar has misled you into lying
A thief has made you steal. Wash out this fleck
Give me the bow, and with it save your name.

ODYSSEUS (*to Neoptolemos*).
You won't help him by doing what he asks
And every moment we waste here will kill
A man of ours upon the field of Troy.

PHILOCTETES.
Then I would tarry here a thousand weeks
Til all the Greeks are slaughtered to a man
In slaughtering the Trojans, their corpses piled
In tottering mounds upon what once was known
As Troy, or by another, Grecian, name
So they can lie a little nearer to
The seat of thunder than the earth, their swords
Shattered, and their broken shields and helms
Crushed beneath the heavens' scornful stars
And all their struggle shrunken to the point
Of who in rotting will most foul the earth.
A moment is worth nothing, it costs a Greek.
What is a Greek? A precious moment's length.
So keep my bow, time lends me better arms.
To kill one Greek I needn't lift a hand.

Another dies, and still I haven't moved.
O Time, thou ageless murderess, ten years
Have I reproached thy unrelenting tread
That never spared my back a single hour
But bent it ever deeper towards the earth
Now quite triumphal seems your course to me
Which lets no living thing escape its march
And knows no limit on its tyranny.
Your course is mine, we march in step together
And both our dwellings lie above the gods.

ODYSSEUS.
The rope.

NEOPTOLEMOS.
                    I must unwillingly refuse
The bow, must unwillingly lend my hand
To bind you, for there is no other way
To free you from this island and yourself.

PHILOCTETES.
Go on like this and you'll have captured nothing
Your ropes will bind thin air, for I'll escape
And dive from this crag to the one below
Borne headlong by my body and my will
Taking the route no living man returns
Less use to you with every rock I strike
And leaving you to scrape from off the stones
A bloodied pulp, and to your rigging bind
A shattered carcass, so you might present
Its foul corruption at your generals' feet
And hold Troy's dogs at bay another hour.
For in their bellies I'll await you there
That when the Trojan dogs tear up your flesh
It will be I who tears it, Philoctetes
Of Melos who on Lemnos did escape
Into the jaws of dogs ahead of you.

ODYSSEUS (*to Neoptolemos*).
Take up his bow, and come with me.
He won't need either it nor us again.
(*To Philoctetes*)
It may be that the breeze from your short fall
Will stiffen Priam's walls against our storm
It may be you'll just steal a narrow lead
On us into the grave, if no god lends
Us aid against the Trojans. Soon or late
And willingly or not, we'll meet our deaths
Perhaps not quite forgotten by the flesh
That rises from the dust that was our own
But Philoctetes armed with a thousand spears
Will tumble to his own oblivion:
A god will sooner lend his aid to us
Than your name will be spoken of again.

PHILOCTETES.
Stay. Don't leave me to the birds a second time.

NEOPTOLEMOS.
Enough of birds. Come with us now. Your bow.

ODYSSEUS.
Give me the bow. An anger so long fed
And nourished thus, does not abate so soon.
Lend him your arm. Mine won't steady him
Along the slanting path, and time is short.

PHILOCTETES.
You steal the bow from me a second time
I'd sooner see it broken in your hands
Than carried by that man, the Ithacan.

ODYSSEUS.
You have denied yourself more than your bow.
Seek solace in your dreams of retribution.

PHILOCTETES.
Are you then offering yourself to me as bait?
It stinks of your dead carcass in the sun.
Go each your way, you neither will return
To Ithaca nor Skyros nor your homes.
And take the bow that I no longer need
Leave me, who won't be used by you again
Give me a sword or axe, or sever off
My legs with it yourself, so they can't go
With you against my will. Tear my head
From off my body that my eyes can't watch
Your sails on the horizon slowly shrink
So you won't hear my voice above the surf
Follow you to the shore and to your ship.
Hack off these hands, before they mutely beg
A place among your oarsmen or your ranks
And tear these arms from off my trunk so they
Cannot be lent to serve a cause I loathe.
What's left, insensible as senseless stone
Won't thwart my will, and I would have it so.

NEOPTOLEMOS.
Leave him to himself. Let him make an end
If life with us seems worse to him than death.

ODYSSEUS.
The three of us have but one life between us.
Come. Let's see what happens when his rage is spent.

Exit Odysseus and Neoptolemos. Pause.
Enter Neoptolemos with the bow.

PHILOCTETES.
What, back with fresher lies or longer rope?

NEOPTOLEMOS.
I wanted to return your bow to you.
Do as you wish, come with us to Troy

Or stay on Lemnos, only now take back
What I when you were helpless took from you:
So what befalls you will not stain my hands
As his have been by what you have endured.

PHILOCTETES.
You wash your hands too late. A change of mind
Changes nothing now. Philoctetes is nothing
Either to himself or you, and nothing's rent
And broken as it falls from crag to crag
If the body torn and broken is my own
And nothing keeps you from the Trojan dogs
Nor lives on Lemnos but the carrion birds
And you, who are so like them. I am nothing
Since I did rid myself of my own self
To rid myself of you who hunted me.
Keep, break or throw away what once was mine.

Enter Odysseus.

ODYSSEUS.
What are you doing with him and with his bow?

NEOPTOLEMOS.
I am returning what you stole from him
With my hands, restoring what we stole
To him we stole it from.

ODYSSEUS.
                                        Give me the bow.

NEOPTOLEMOS.
You of all men will not stop me in this.

ODYSSEUS.
You're giving away your life and my life with it.

NEOPTOLEMOS.
I would not owe my life to such a crime.

ODYSSEUS.
Not only yours, but his and many others.

NEOPTOLEMOS.
Death spares the gods alone. Men must not lie.

ODYSSEUS.
Had you but borne your lies a little longer.
We would have had a tide beneath our keel
With sea enough to wash away this stain
For you need neither your blood nor our own
To cleanse your hands, and we'd be bound for Troy
And he a few short days from being cured.
A stone had better served me in this cause
Deaf to the voice by years of silence sweetened
And blind to the face that exile and disease
Has made into a mask of what it was.
Why did I leave unstoppped your eyes and ears.
Return to me his bow, his other weapon
Before his wound has prised it from your grip
And go back to the ship and stir the waves
And if you've tears to shed beweep the fish
Because the gods refused to grant them wings
Or else the ship, because its timbers now
Are leafless and will never put forth buds
And wait for him to want to live again.
For we have gone so far in this affair
And spread the net between us so far wide
That only by proceeding can we leave.
Spit out your pity, for it tastes of blood
There's no place here for virtue, and no time
Don't ask about the gods, you live with men
Of gods you'll learn enough when time allows.

NEOPTOLEMOS (*to Philoctetes*).
Take it, before he sways me once again.

ODYSSEUS.
Get back, or else I'll feed the birds your arm

NEOPTOLEMOS.
Or I your tongue the fishes.

Neoptolemos drops the bow. Swordfight.
Philoctetes picks up the bow.

PHILOCTETES.
                                                                    Stop.

(*To Neoptolemos*)
Drop your sword. I want him in one piece.
(*To Odysseus*)
You'd cut him into pieces. I don't hate him
And therefore wouldn't mourn him if he died.
Drop your sword, so you don't scratch yourself
Before I do. Your death is now my task
And I accept it willingly. Would we were
Immortal, and I could grant eternal death.

NEOPTOLEMOS.
Your hate shows that you loved what he stole from you
Now duty's brought him here to give it back.

PHILOCTETES.
How fluently these words trip off your tongue.
You speak of someone I no longer am.
These rocks are better listeners than I
Perhaps they'll lend your voice an ear before
I stop its whining.

NEOPTOLEMOS.
                                With the bow that I
Returned to you, believing what you were.

PHILOCTETES.
With the same.

ODYSSEUS.
                         Then let me tell you, No Man,
Who you were. Our way to Troy out of the storm.
The sea god in his ancient envy shook
Our fleet, those wooden hulks that swam across
His watery sky, and hungered to devour
Us, alien creatures of another world:
His swollen clouds heaved up the waves against us
The selfsame clouds then beat us back with rain
The tempest drove our ships upon each other
So mast upon mast, bulwark on bulwark crashed
While on our decks Poseidon seized the helm
Steering in circles, drawing his surging tides
And driving winds that in a vortex caught
Our stricken fleet, and made the howling seas
A safer haven than the longed-for shore.
And yet we found we could not sacrifice
To the raging god, for coiled about the shrine
A serpent writhed. What every man refused
You did, and bore its bite, and cleared the way
To Troy by making offer of your foot.
Again the sea god cast his eye on us
And stifling his breath becalmed the sea
The calm held us more firmly than the storm
Our thirty sails hung slack, and once again
We could not sacrifice, but now the cause
Was you, to whom the other rite was due
Your howls disturbed the solemn ritual
And so your foot condemned you to this shore.
Now I would set you free from this exile
And grant you a long-deserved eternal fame.
By killing me you kill three thousand men
And those three thousand dead will Troy preserve
And Troy preserved will mean our cities' doom.
You think you set your foot upon my neck
It is the very earth that holds you up

If I should never see my home again
You will not either, I am your native land
Its fields and pastures live and die with me.

PHILOCTETES.
Are your jaws working still, does your tongue writhe
In hope of snatching some last shreds of time?
Can you not hear the silence crush your words.
What do I care of cities, is there one here?
They're less than nothing to me. Nor do I
Believe in them. They're built of words and dreams
Are traps laid in the air by sightless eyes.
They sprout from fevered minds where lies with lies
Have other lies engendered, lies as well
What you call fields and pastures. Desolate
Is my world, and I would make your own the same
A something that's been hung between two voids
Eviscerated by the idle gods
A creature of its own entrails' corruption
Til washed by fire stolen from the gods
It draws from that corruption its own power
Voided of everything when the void reclaims
The stars it lent to time. Tear out your eyes
They lie, their empty sockets speak the truth
The only truth left my life is your death.

ODYSSEUS.
And yet disaster might still be escaped
If not by us prevailing then by you.
The laurels can't be tasted by the dead.
Each word I speak is coloured by my death
Which you hold in your hand, my name upon
My own lips in the shadow of your bow
Tastes but of blood. Follow this boy to Troy
And leave my body here. He had no part
In that wrong done to you so long ago

And lent his hand today unwillingly.
At Troy invent a death for me that will
Keep my men in the war and make my grave
Unfindable, whether it should be
A fish devoured me because it craved my voice
Or else a sea god, because I bespat the waves.

NEOPTOLEMOS (*standing in front of him*).
I gave away the bow. Now let me be
Your shield.
(*To Philoctetes*)
              Take my life for his.
(*To Odysseus*)
                            It must be
Less use to both of you.

ODYSSEUS.
Til you can be some help stay out of this.

PHILOCTETES.
You heard him. And I myself shall need your face
As a mirror, so that when I put him out
I'll watch it in your eyes before I put
You out yourself. Why did the god refuse
To grant me eyes to watch my own eyes watching
Why did he make a moment's span so short?
Could I but tear the last thing that he sees
From out your eyes, his last howls from your ears.
(*To Odysseus.*)
Now learn your duty to the generals' cause
Marooned upon a rock with rotting foot
Which forces you to crawl about that rock
Fleeing upon three legs the stinking fourth
That can't be fled, fleeing your own howls
That can't be fled, that fleeing hurts the more
And louder, should you stop you ears, inside
Your head, drunk from your own stink, a carrion

Set out for vultures, shrinking inside them
A dunghill for the vultures, soon to be
Their dung yourself, struggling to outcrawl
Your own decay, that's eaten up your foot
And soon will you, however fast you crawl.
Do you know how to shriek? We teach it here.
Can you suck vulture's bones? Here's where you'll learn.
So taste your harvest, fields and pastures green
Before I tear you from you by your roots.
(*Shoots a vulture, and throws it to Odysseus.*)
Your vulture. Learn from me what you have taught.
Eat. It's eaten others like you, soon it will
Feed on you, so be nourished from your grave
That it can nourish others once you're dead.
What, does your task revolt you?

NEOPTOLEMOS.
                                        I know mine does.
(*He picks up the sword and runs it through Philoctetes' back.*)
I never thought I'd kill a man this way
Driving a route to Hades through his back.
I would some other hand had quenched his life.
Sad fame it is, to kill a man who's dead.
His blood escapes the carcass of his death
Which his corrupted foot claimed years ago.
I have expunged the wrongs we did to him
And he did us.

ODYSSEUS.
                    You learn your lessons quickly.

NEOPTOLEMOS.
What shadow blots the day?

ODYSSEUS.
                                        The vulture nation
Is gathering to performing its final task.

Bring rocks.
(*Neoptolemos brings rocks.*)
What's left from what we've done to him and what
Won't last, must never find its way into
The vultures' bellies, where the flesh won't know
Where all its different parts are billeted
The breast lodged with the neck, the foot the scalp
Let's hide with rocks what I left on this rock.
(*They do so.*)
Leave out the bow, he won't need it again
I doubt the vultures will devour it.
I do not gladly owe my life his death.

NEOPTOLEMOS.
Nor was it gladly given. And not for long.
That empty hand once bore a thousand spears.

ODYSSEUS.
It makes no difference now. Take up the bow.

NEOPTOLEMOS.
You told me if he didn't come with us
Then Troy would raze our cities to the ground.

ODYSSEUS.
I did. And now I'm telling you something else.
Which is, this man we needed in seven storms
We need no longer, and must be left behind
Beneath these rocks, with both his feet now healed
And we without him must conclude the war.
Take up his quiver too, we'll need it there.
I would some god would let me join his sleep.
O thunder, roll the sky from out my sight
O lightning, cleave the earth beneath my feet.
But nothing happens. Let us go then and exchange
The earth's unsteady footing for the waves
And for the sight of this half-buried corpse

The countless bodies buried on the plain
That isn't wide enough to hold them all
Too quickly and too many have been killed
And yet not soon enough and not too many.
The city won't be ours til mounds of dead
Overtop its walls. So let us leave at once
Before the god in earnest takes my prayer
And sends me to my sleep on sombre wings
And we must sail back home one killer less
To the coast we've washed with blood these last ten years.
(*He goes, stops.*)
But though we didn't catch the fish alive
His body might be useful as a bait.
Perhaps it's just as well he can't prevent
His wound from being used to sway his men.
Remove the stones. I'll take him on my back
And carrying him I'll lend his corpse my feet.
(*They do so.*)
You were a greater burden to me living
Ten years I bore you, and with your weight this rock
Now those ten famished years have lightened you.
(*Turning to Neoptolemos.*)
We'll say the Trojans reached the isle before us
In hope they could enlist him for their side.
But he would not betray the Grecian cause
And for his loyalty they murdered him
Enraged they couldn't purchase him with gold
Nor arguments or threats. And so he died
Before our eyes, as we approached the shore
And struggled in our vessel with the surf
By seven Trojans circled, while an eighth
Ran through his back a sword, we heard his cry
Above the roar, and saw his body fall
The sight of which did send you to a rage.
A wave swept us that very instant, tore
The rudder from your hands and nearly cast

Our boat upon the rocks, while its retreat
Swiftly bore the enemy away
Beneath our readied spears to open sea
Where they in a light-masted skiff set sail
While we were still belaboured by the waves
Whose violence had robbed us of revenge.
The killers left the bow in hurried flight
And we saw all their faces, their cowardice
Proven by the wound that scores his back.

NEOPTOLEMOS.
If he can be dispensed with, so can you.
I followed you and trampled underfoot
The best in me, turned liar, killer, thief
I saw the Trojan and I saw him kill
Two men.

ODYSSEUS (*turns around, with the dead man on his back*).
          Then let me lend you my dead back.
Shoot, and lend some credence to your lies.
And know that if the Trojans kill me here
I cannot act as witness to your tale
There's little we can say about each other
That men believe, and nothing that you can.
Three thousand know from your mouth and from mine
Your hate for me, who bears your father's arms
The bow that's justly yours by law of battle
When you killed him that bore it, you now draw
Against yourself. And your arrow flies
Back to you as swiftly as the stones
Your men will fling when they learn of your lies.
A good shield is a borrowed hide, a better
A dead man round your neck, your hatred clads
Me in iron.
(*He turns back.*)

NEOPTOLEMOS (*puts away the arrow*).
                    Would it were otherwise.

ODYSSEUS.
Change your burden with mine.
(*They do so. Odysseus takes the bow, Neoptolemos the dead
    body.*)
                                        Go on ahead.
At Troy you'll learn the lies you'd need to tell
To clear yourself of killing me right here.
(*They leave, Neoptolemos going ahead.*)
Husband your rage, don't let it go to waste.
At Troy a feast awaits you. Now go on.

Playwright's Notes

1 An interval may be held after Odysseus' and Neoptolemos' first
exit. During the interval, with the house doors open and the house
lights up, two clowns (the actors playing Odysseus and Neoptolemos)
fight with wooden swords. The audience will be able to stay or leave,
watch or not, as they choose.

2 After Odysseus and Neoptolemos have made their last exit with
Philoctetes' body, images from military history could be projected
onto a screen, from the Trojan War down to the war in the Pacific.

THE HORATIAN

Then the cities of Rome and Alba
Fought for dominion. While against them both
Stood the Etruscans, armed in great array.
So faced with common threat the two drew up
In ranks against each other to end their strife
Before the foe attacked. Their generals each
Came forth before their armies and said one
To the other: Since battle can only weaken
Victor and vanquished, let us cast lots
So one man may fight for our city
Against another fighting for your own
Sparing the others for the common foe
And the armies beat their swords against their shields
As sign of their assent and the lots were cast.
And the lots determined that there should fight
A Horatian for Rome, a Curiatian for Alba.
The Curiatian was betrothed to the Horatian's sister
And the Horatian and the Curiatian
Were asked, each by his own side:

He is   your
            betrothed to   sister
You are   his

Should the lots
Be cast again?
And the Horatian and the Curiatian said: No
And they fought among the assembled ranks
And the Horatian wounded the Curiatian
And the Curiatian cried with faltering voice:
Spare the vanquished. I am
Betrothed to your sister.
And the Horatian cried:
My bride is Rome
And the Horatian thrust his sword
Through the Curiatian's throat, so that the blood spilt
    upon the earth.
And when unscathed his comrades bore him home
Upon their shields, and he had slung the shirt
Of the Curiatian he'd killed across his shoulder
And from his belt had hung the dead man's sword
As a trophy, in his hands his bloodied own
His sister met him at the eastern gate
With hurried steps, and behind her slowly came
His aged father
And to the people's joy the victor leapt
From the shields to receive his sister's embrace.
But his sister saw at once the bloody tunic
That she herself had made, and wailed and tore her hair.
And the Horatian reproached his sister for her grief:
Why do you wail and tear your hair?
Rome is victorious. Before you stands the victor.
And his sister kissed the bloody shirt and cried:
Rome.
Return to me who once this tunic bore.
And the Horatian, his arm still taut
From the blow with which he'd killed the Curiatian
For whom his sister wept
Thrust his sword on which the dead man's blood
Had not yet dried

Into her weeping breast, so that the blood
Spilt upon the earth. He said:
Now go to him whom you love more than Rome.
This for every woman
That mourns the enemy.
And showed the Romans the twice-bloodied sword
And the cheering fell silent. Only from the back
Of the assembled crowd could still be heard
Shouts of joy, where the atrocity
Had not been witnessed. When his father
Arrived amid the silent crowd he had
Just one child left. He said:
You have killed your sister.
And the Horatian did not hide the twice-bloodied sword
And the Horatian's father
Looked upon the twice-bloodied sword and said:
You are victorious. Rome
Rules over Alba.
Then covered his face and wept for his daughter
And spread upon her wounds the tunic
That she herself had made, by the same sword
Bloodied, and embraced the victor.
Then the lictors
Came forth and with their bundled axe and rods
Parted the embrace of father and son
And took the dead man's sword from the victor's belt
And from the murderer's hand his own
Twice bloodied.
And from among the Romans one called out:
He is victorious. Rome
Rules over Alba.
And from among the Romans another replied:
He has killed his sister.
And the Romans cried out against each other:
Honour the victor
Punish the murderer.

And Romans against Romans took up swords
In quarrel as to whether
The Horatian be honoured as a victor
Or punished as a murderer. The lictors
Parted the opposing sides with bundled axe and rods
And called upon the people to assemble
And from their midst the people elected two
Who would pass judgement on the Horatian
And gave to one a wreath of laurels
With which to crown the victor
And to the other an axe
With which to punish the murderer
And between crown and axe
Stood the Horatian.
But his father, the most of all bereft, now stood
Beside his son and said:
This folly shames us, Alba itself
Could not have witnessed it without shame.
Against the city stand the Etruscans
And Rome would break her best sword.
You think of only one life.
Think of Rome.
And from among the Romans one replied:
Rome has many swords.
No Roman
Is less than Rome, or there can be no Rome.
And from among the Romans another spoke
And pointed with his finger at the foe:
Twice as mighty
Are the Etruscans when Rome is set
Against itself
By many voices
In untimely dispute.
And the first replied:
Words unspoken
Burden the sword arm.

Contention hidden
Weakens the ranks for war.
And for a second time the lictors parted
From the Horatian those who would embrace him, and
    the Romans each
Drew their swords.
The one who bore the laurels and the one who bore the
    axe each
Drew their swords, so that they held
In their left hands the laurels or the axe and in their right
Their swords. The lictors themselves
Set aside the symbols of their office
A moment long and each one thrust their sword
Into their belts and took
Up again the bundled rods and axe
And the Horatian stooped
To retrieve his bloodied sword from the dust. But the lic-
    tors
Stopped him with their bundled rods and axe.
And the father of the Horatian drew his sword and with
    his left hand
Stooped to lift the victor murderer's bloodied own
And the lictors stopped him too
And the guards were doubled at the four gates
And the dispute resumed
As they awaited the enemy.
And the one who bore the laurels said:
His service quits his crime.
And the one who bore the axe said:
His crime undoes his service.
And the one who bore the laurels asked:
Should the victor be punished?
And the one who bore the axe asked:
Should the murderer be honoured?
And the one who bore the laurels said:
If the murderer is punished

The victor is punished.
And the one who bore the axe said:
If the victor is honoured
The murderer is honoured.
And the people looked upon him
That had committed the two deeds, one man, indivisible
And were silent.
And the one who bore the laurels and the one who bore
    the axe asked:
If the one cannot be done
Without being undone by the other

                    victor   murderer
Because the   and the   are one man, indivisible
            murderer   victor

Should we then do neither

                    victory   victor
And let there be a   without a
                    murder   murderer
                    victor
Or rather call the   no one?
                    murderer

And the people replied with one voice
(Though the father of the Horatian was silent):
Behold the victor. His name: Horatius.
Behold the murderer. His name: Horatius.
In one man live many men.
One has won victory for Rome.
Another has killed his sister
Needlessly. Let each receive his due.
To the victor the laurels. To the murderer the axe.
And the Horatian was crowned with the laurels
And he who'd borne them held aloft his sword
And with his arm outstretched honoured the victor
And the lictors set aside
Their bundled rods and axe and from the dust

Took up the sword twice stained with different bloods
And gave it to the victor
And crowned with laurels the Horatian held
Aloft his sword so all the Romans saw
Its blade twice stained with different bloods
And he who bore the axe set it aside, and the Romans all
Held aloft their swords with arms outstretched
And for the space of three heartbeats
Honoured the victor.
Then the lictors thrust their swords
Back into their belts, and took
The victor's sword from the murderer's hand and threw it
Back into the dust where it had been, and he who bore the
    axe
Tore from the victor's brow the laurels that
Had crowned the murderer and gave them back
To him who'd borne them and cast over the Horatian's
    head
The cloth dyed black as the night
To which he'd been condemned
Because he needlessly had killed
And the Romans all
Thrust their swords into their scabbards
So that all the blades were covered
And the weapons that had honoured the victor
Would not witness the murderer's punishment. But the
    guards
At the four gates awaiting the enemy
Did not cover their swords
And the blades of the axes and the victor's sword
Lying bloody in the dust, they too remained uncovered.
And the father of the Horatian said:
This child is my last. Let me die for him.
And the people answered with one voice:
No man can be another man
And justice was performed upon the Horatian

So that his blood spilt upon the earth
And he who'd borne the laurels raised again
The broken crown that from the murderer's head
Was roughly torn, and asked:
What shall be done with the victor's corpse?
And the people answered with one voice:
The victor's corpse should be borne aloft
Upon the shields of those his sword has saved.
And they put together as best they could
What never could again be reassembled
The murderer's head and the murderer's body
Divided by the executioner's axe
And bloodied by both, and bore the victor's corpse
Upon the shields of those his sword had saved
Heedless to his blood that stained their shields
Heedless to his blood upon their hands
Then crowned him with the laurels they had torn
From off his brow
And closed his rigid fingers round the hilt
Of his bloodied dirtied sword
And crossed their naked swords above the corpse
To signify that never the remains
Of him that had won victory for Rome
Should suffer injury from rain nor time
Nor snow nor oblivion from human memory
And covering their faces mourned him.
But the guards at the four gates
Awaiting the enemy
Did not cover their faces.
And he who'd borne the axe who bore again
In his hands the axe
On which the victor's blood had not yet dried
Asked the people:
What shall be done with the murderer's corpse?
And the people replied with one voice
(Though the last of the Horatii was silent):

The murderer's corpse
Should be thrown to the dogs
To be torn apart
So that nothing will remain of him
That needlessly has killed.
And the last Horatian, his face
Twice stained with tears, said:
The victor is dead, never to be forgotten
So long as Rome shall rule over Alba.
Forget the murderer as I, who am the most bereft
Have forgotten him.
And from among the Romans one replied:
Longer than Rome shall rule over Alba
Shall his Rome be remembered and the example
It has given or not given
Weighing one against the other in the scales
Or cleanly marking service from the crime
In what one man, indivisible, had done
Fearing the impure truth or not fearing it
For half of an example is no example
What is not taken to its proper end
In course of time crawls crablike to oblivion.
And the crown was taken off the victor's head
And from among the Romans one came forth
And bowed before the body, and said:
Now with your permission we will tear
From your unfeeling hand this sword we need.
And from among the Romans another came and spat upon
  the corpse and said:
Murderer, give up the sword.
And the sword was torn from his hand
For rigid in death that hand
Had closed around the hilt
So that they had to break the Horatian's fingers
Before he would give up the weapon
With which he'd killed for Rome and once

Not for Rome, bloodied once too often
So what he had used well and once used ill
Could be better used by others.
And rent in pieces by the executioner's axe
The murderer's corpse was thrown to the dogs
And they tore it apart, leaving nothing
Of him who so needlessly had killed
Or as good as nothing.
And then the Romans asked among themselves:
How shall he be remembered by our heirs?
And the people replied with one voice:
He shall be called the victor over Alba
He shall be called the killer of his sister
In one breath both his service and his crime.
And he who speaks of his crime and not his service
Shall doglike live among the dogs
And he who speaks of his service and not his crime
He too shall live among the dogs.
But he who speaks of his crime one time
And of his service another
The same mouth speaking differently at different times
Or differently for different ears
He shall have his tongue torn out.
For our words must remain pure. For
A sword can be broken and a man
Can also be broken, but words
Fall irrevocably into the workings of the world
Leaving things knowable or unknowable.
And lethal to us is what we cannot know.
Thus waiting for the enemy they feared
The impure truth no longer as they set
An example of pure division for the future
Not hiding the remainder that could not
Be unmade by the world's unceasing change
And each went back to work, bearing together
With hammers, ploughs, awls and quills, their swords.

Playwright's Note

The performance follows the action described in the text. (ALL ACTORS: Then the cities of Rome . . . before the foe attacked. *Allocation of dialogue.* THE GENERALS: Their generals each / Came forth before their armies and said one / To the other: because battle will only weaken, etc. Variation: THE GENERALS: Their generals each / Came forth before their armies and said one / To the other. ALL ACTORS: Because battle will only weaken . . .). *All props*: masks (masks for Romans and Albanians, a mask for the sister, dog masks), weapons, etc., remain visible throughout the performance. No one exits the stage. Any actor who has spoken all his lines and finished his performance returns to his starting position or changes his role. (Following the battle, the Albanians play the Roman people receiving the victor. Following the murder, two Roman soldiers play the lictors, etc.) After each killing an actor comes to the front of the stage and drops a red cloth. After he is killed, the actor playing the Horatian can be replaced by a doll. The doll should be over life size. The text that begins: And rigid in death that hand . . . should always be spoken by the actor who plays the Horatian.

MAUSER

CHORUS.
You fought at the front in the Civil War
The enemy found no weakness in you
We have found no weakness in you
Now you are yourself a weakness
In us that the enemy must not find.
In Vitebsk on our orders you destroyed
Enemies of the Revolution in the town
Knowing the Revolution's daily bread
In Vitebsk as in cities everywhere
Is its enemies' death, knowing
Grass must be torn up if it is to grow
We killed by your hand. And yet one day
You killed without our orders those who were
To us no enemies by that same hand
And must yourself die, enemy to us.
The Revolution's put you at a post
You will not leave alive, against a wall
That is to be your last, do your duty
As you have done so many times before
Knowing the Revolution's daily bread
In Vitebsk as in cities everywhere

Is its' enemies death, knowing
Grass must be torn up if it is to grow.

A.
I've done my duty.

CHORUS.
Do your last.

A.
I've killed for the Revolution.

CHORUS.
Die for it.

A.
I've made a mistake.

CHORUS.
You are the mistake.

A.
I'm human.

CHORUS.
What is that.

A.
I don't want to die.

CHORUS.
We are not asking if you want to die.
You stand with your back to the last wall
You will stand with your back to. You are not
Needed by the Revolution any more,
Your death is. But until you lend your Yes
To the No that's been pronounced upon your life
You haven't done your duty. Here before
The Revolution's rifles that require

Your death, learn your last lesson. That lesson is:
You against the wall are your own enemy and ours.

A.
PROLETARIANS OF ALL THE WORLD UNITE
Words read in secret, hid under desks at school
And kept behind the cistern in the jakes
Were written with boot heels and rifle butts
By prison guards from Odessa to Omsk
On this, the little seminary boy's
Flesh, the tradesman's son who had his own
Samovar, and knelt for hours in prayer
Before Our Lady, assiduously prepared
For a calling that I couldn't leave too soon.
The meetings, protests, demonstrations, strikes
When Cossacks charged the crowd and cut us down
With righteous zeal or marched us off to jails
Where bored officials beat us listlessly:
These taught me nothing of an afterlife.
The war taught me to kill, when our brigade
Surrounded saw the choice could only be
To kill or to be killed, well then I killed
We'd say: Who does not kill he will not eat
Who will not bayonet an officer
A peasant or Cadet who haven't grasped
The truths we know. We said it was a job
Like any other, breaking human skulls.

A (CHORUS).
And yet one morning in Vitebsk with noise
Of battle near the Revolution gave
Me the order to assume command
Of the revolutionary tribunal in Vitebsk
And liquidate the Revolution's enemies.

CHORUS.
You fought at the front in the Civil War
The enemy found no weakness in you
We have found no weakness in you.
Leave the front and take up the post
The Revolution now requires of you
Until it needs you elsewhere. Lead the fight
In our rear, liquidate our enemies.

A (CHORUS).
And I approved the terms of this commission.
Knowing the Revolution's daily bread
Is its enemies' death, knowing
Grass must be torn up if it is to grow
I approved the terms of this commission
Assigned me in the noise of battle by
The Revolution with the Party's voice.
And this killing was a different kind of killing
And this work was unlike any other work.

CHORUS.
Your work begins today. Your predecessor
Must die before tomorrow, an enemy himself.

A.
Why him.

B.
Three peasants stood before me, enemies
Of the Revolution out of ignorance.
The hands behind their backs bound with ropes
Were calloused with work, and bound to my hand
By the Revolution's task my revolver was
Pointing at their necks. I knew their enemies
Were mine and only they who faced the pit
Did not, but I who knew had nothing else
To teach them with than my revolver's bullet.

In Vitebsk I'd killed many enemies
Knowing the Revolution's daily bread
Is its enemies' death, knowing
Grass must be torn up if it is to grow
Knowing the Revolution kills by my own hand.
But now I only knew I could not kill.
The task the Revolution issued me
By order of the Party in Vitebsk
With noise of battle near I now resigned
And cut the rope that bound the hands of our
Three enemies that had been worn by work
Like my hands, like the hands of those I loved.
Your enemies, I said, are ours as well
Remember that. Now go back to your work.

CHORUS (ACTORS PLAYING THE THREE PEASANTS).
And they went back to work, three enemies
Of the Revolution who had learned nothing.
When he resigned the task assigned to him
By order of the Party in Vitebsk
One morning with the noise of battle near
His hand became another at our throat.
For your hand isn't yours no more than mine
Is mine until the Revolution's won
In Vitebsk as in cities everywhere.
For ignorance can kill no less than guns
Or fever and to know is not enough
But ignorance must end at last for good
And killing is a science that must be
Mastered if it ever is to stop
For what's natural isn't natural, but we
Must tear the grass and spit out the bread
Until the Revolution finally wins
In Vitebsk as in cities everywhere
And grass grows back and men no longer starve.
For he who claims to own himself is just

Another enemy of the Revolution
And our friends are not our friends no more than we
Are we ourselves, nor is the Revolution one
With itself, but the enemy still carves
With tooth and claw, bayonet and gun
Its loathsome features on our living face
And covers it with scars.

B.
Why kill then
If the price of the revolution is the Revolution
Or that of freedom, those we would free

A.
That or something like it he cried out
Above the noise of battle that had grown
And still grew. At our throat a thousand hands
Against this doubt no remedy except
The doubter's death. Then when he stood before me
And faced the pit, I didn't see his hands
Nor whether work had calloused them or not
Only that they were tightly bound with ropes
And so we killed him by my hand that day
Knowing the Revolution's daily bread
Is its' enemies death, knowing
Grass must be torn up if it is to grow.
This I knew on the next day when I killed
And killing on the third day knew it still
And those I killed had neither hands nor face
Only the eye with which I looked at them
Only the mouth with which I spoke to them
Which was my gun and bullets were my words
And when they screamed and fell into the pit
And piled upon each other, enemies
Upon enemies, I did not forget
It was a job like any other job.
I knew that when you shoot a human being

He bleeds like any animal, that little
Distinguishes the dead and that little
Doesn't last long. Only a human being
Isn't an animal: on the seventh day
I saw their faces, tied behind their backs
Their hands, some calloused with a lifetime's work
Some not, and while they stood and faced the pit
And waited for the death that I'd supply
By my revolver a space for doubt appeared
Between my hand and trigger, loading the weight
Of seven days' dead upon my neck which bore
The Revolution's yoke so every other
Yoke might be broken, and upon my hand
Bound to its revolver by the Revolution's task
Given one morning in Vitebsk with noise
Of battle near, the Party's order for
Its enemies to be killed in order that
Killing stop for ever, and I spoke then
The command that day as on the very first
DEATH TO THE ENEMIES OF THE REVOLUTION
And then supplied it, but my voice that spoke
The command wasn't like my voice, nor did the hand
That issued death seem like my hand to me
And the killing was like none other on that day
And the work was like none other. That evening in
The mirror that was cracked for every time
The city had been taken I saw my face
Stare back at me with eyes that weren't my own
That night I wasn't human any more:
The dead of seven days weighed on my neck
My prick became a gun supplying death
To enemies lined up before a pit.

A (CHORUS).
Why me. Relieve me from this task that I've
Become too weak for.

CHORUS.
Why you.

A.
I fought at the front in the Civil War
The enemy found no weakness in me
You have found no weakness in me
Now I am myself a weakness
In us that the enemy must not find.
In Vitebsk I was ordered to destroy
Enemies of the Revolution in Vitebsk
Knowing the Revolution's daily bread
In Vitebsk as in cities everywhere
Is its enemies' death, knowing
Grass must be torn up if it is to grow.
I knew this on the third day and the seventh
But by the tenth I could no longer grasp
What it could mean, when every third I killed
Might not be guilty, standing at the pit
And waiting for the death that I'd supply.

CHORUS.
Because this struggle will not end until
We beat them or are beaten each of us
In Vitebsk as in cities everywhere
Must do the work of two thousand hands with two
Weak hands, hands crushed and bound with chains and
    ropes
Hands cut off, hands clutching at our throats.
A thousand hands are clutching at our throats
And we've no breath to spare to ask the guilt
Or innocence of each hand at our throat
Nor whose they are nor whether they have been
Calloused with work nor whether it was want
And ignorance of what had caused that want
That forced them to our throats or whether it was fear

Of the Revolution that would tear out that want
By the roots. So tell us how are you
Any different from us or more unique
To stand upon your weakness. The I that speaks
With your mouth is not you but someone else.
And not until the Revolution's won
In Vitebsk as in cities everywhere
Will you own who you are. The Revolution
Kills by your hand. You kill by all the hands
The Revolution kills with. Your weakness
Is our weakness, your conscience will remain
A gap within your thinking that becomes
A gap within our front. Who are you.

A.
A soldier of the Revolution.

CHORUS.
Then would you have
The Revolution relieve you from the task
For which you are too weak and which must be
Performed by someone else if not by you.

A (CHORUS).
No.
And the killing went on, and others came
To face the pit and die. And the next day
A peasant stood before me just as those
Like him had stood on other days and just
As those like me had stood elsewhere before
Other gunmen, and on his neck I saw
The sweat of fear: we knew he had betrayed
Four comrades to our enemy and his
Who'd stood before those gunmen, sweating fear.
My enemies are his and they have killed
Those like him for the last two thousand years
As they've killed those like me, with noose and knout

With gallows wheels and irons with knife and axe
And now my gun is pointing at his neck
And now I am wheels gallows noose and knout
I am the gun that's pointing at my neck
Knowing that the Revolution kills
By my hand, crushing gallows noose and knout
And not knowing, before my gun a man
And trapped between my hand and gun I am
The gap that's in my thinking, in our front.

CHORUS.
Your task was never killing human beings
But enemies. The fact is we don't know
What a human being is. We only know
That killing is a job that must be done
But a human being's more than just his job.
For not until the Revolution's won
In Vitebsk as in cities everywhere
Shall we know what a human being is.
The human is our work, for we expose
What's hid behind the masks or buried deep
In the filth of its own history, the face beneath
The leprous sores, the living core within
The fossil, for the Revolution tears
The masks from off the faces, obliterates
The body's leprous sores and washes off
With bayonet and gun, with tooth and knout
The filth encrusted over what is human
Which rising from the chain of generations
And tearing off its bloody navelcord
And recognizing in the lightning flash
Of true beginnings its own self and those
Like it, each one according to its kind
Tears the human from the human by the roots.
For death means nothing, what counts is the example.

A.
But in the noise of battle that had grown
And still grew I still stood with bloody hands
A soldier and a weapon of the Revolution
And with my voice I asked for certainty.

A (CHORUS).
When the Revolution's won will killing stop.
And will it win. How much longer still.

CHORUS.
You know what we know, we know what you know.
The Revolution wins or there won't be
Any human beings: they'll disappear beneath
An implacable humanity.

A.
And I heard my own voice saying
That morning as on every other morning
DEATH TO THE ENEMIES OF THE REVOLUTION
And I saw the thing I was kill something else
Of flesh and blood and other matter, not
Asking for its guilt or innocence
Nor for its name nor whether in fact it was
An enemy or not, and after it lay still
The thing I was did not stop killing it
It said: (CHORUS) My burden is cast off: the dead
No longer weigh upon my neck. A man
Is something that you shoot until that man
Arises from the rubble of himself.
And after it had shot it many times
And watched the bursting skin spew bloody flesh
And splintered bones it sanctioned what it did
By trampling with its feet upon the corpse.

A (CHORUS).
I take beneath my heels what I have killed

And dance on it to pound its face to pulp
For I am not content to kill what must
Die if the Revolution is to win
And killing end, but it must disappear
From the face of the earth forever, leaving behind
A new world for the generations to come.

CHORUS.
We heard him howl and saw what he had done
Without our orders and that he would not stop
Screaming with the human voice of one
Who preys on human beings. Then we knew
That his work had used him up and that his time
Was over and we led him off as we
Would any enemy of the Revolution
And not like any, but his own enemy too
Knowing the Revolution's daily bread
Is its enemies' death, knowing
Grass must be torn up if it is to grow.
For he'd cast off the burden he must bear
Til the Revolution's victory, and the dead
No longer weighed upon his shoulders, to be borne
Until the Revolution's victory, for his burden
Was now his prey and the Revolution had
No place for him any more, no more than he
Had any place for himself except the one
Before the rifles of the Revolution.

A.
And only when they took me from my work
And took away my gun, my fingers still
Bent around the weapon that had been
A part of me, did I see what I'd done
And not until they led me off could I
Hear my voice and again the mounting noise
Of battle that grew louder all about.

A (CHORUS).
Now my own kind have led me to the wall
And I who understood no longer can.
Why.

CHORUS.
You know what we know, we know what you know.
Your work was bloody, unlike any other
And yet like any other must be done
By one of us or other.

A.
I did my duty.
Look, my hand.

CHORUS.
We see your hand is bloody.

A.
As it must be.
And louder than the noise of battle was
The silence in Vitebsk for that short time
And longer than a lifetime. I'm human.
A human's not a machine. To kill and kill
And still remain the same with every death
I could not do. Let me sleep like a machine.

CHORUS.
Not until the Revolution's won
In Vitebsk as in cities everywhere
Shall we know what a human being is.

A.
I must know here and now. I who am led
To death this morning in Vitebsk, the blood
Still on my boots, I whose time has run
Do ask the Revolution here and now
What is the thing we call a human being.

CHORUS.
You ask too soon. We cannot help you now.
Nor does your question help the Revolution.
You hear the noise of battle.

A.
I have just this one time.
And silence waits beyond the noise of battle
Like a black snow.

CHORUS.
You die only once
But many deaths the Revolution dies.
And many times it has, and none too many.
And either human beings will become
More than just their work or there won't be
Any human beings. You no longer are
Your work has used you up and you must be
Erased from off the surface of the earth.
The blood you stained your hand with when it was
The Revolution's hand must now be washed
With your blood in the Revolution's name
Which needs the hands of all men, saving yours.

A.
I killed on your orders.

CHORUS.
And without our orders.
The second's lapse between your hand and trigger
Was ours and yours. The space between your gun
And you was your position at the front
Of the Revolution. But when that hand became
One with the gun then you also became
One with your work and lost all thinking then
Of how that work needs doing here and now
So that it never need be done again

By anyone, and then your post became
A gap in our front and there no longer was
Any place in it for you. For habit is
Loathsome, and deadly what comes naturally
The past still strikes deep roots in us and must
Be torn out by the roots. The dead arise
In our weakness and we must bury them again
And again, must ourselves give up our selves
Only each other we must never give up.
You are both the one man and the other
The one you mangled beneath your boots
The one who mangled you beneath your boots
Each of you have given up the other
Only the Revolution hasn't given you up.
Learn how to die. We learn from what you learn.
Die learning. Don't give up the Revolution.

A.
I refuse.
I reject my death. My life is mine.

CHORUS.
Nothing is yours.

A (CHORUS).
I don't want to die. I'll clutch the ground and bury
Myself in it, eat mouthfuls of the earth
I do not choose to leave. I'll scream.

CHORUS (A).
We know
The work it takes to die. Your fear is yours.

A (CHORUS).
What comes after death.

CHORUS (A).
He asked again and presently got up

No longer screaming, and we answered him:
You know what we know, we know what you know
And your question doesn't help the Revolution.
If your life could be an answer it might be
Permitted. But the Revolution needs
Your approval on your death. He asked no more
But stood and faced the wall and gave the command
Knowing the Revolution's daily bread
Is its enemies' death, knowing
Grass must be torn up if it is to grow.

A (CHORUS).
DEATH TO THE ENEMIES OF THE REVOLUTION

Playwright's Note

Written in 1970 as the third play in an experimental series, of which
the first was PHILOCTETES and the second THE HORATIAN,
MAUSER examines/criticizes the theory and practice of Brecht's
LEHRSTÜCKE.[1] A variation on a theme from Sholokhov's *Quiet
Flows the Don*, MAUSER is not a repertory play; it takes an extreme
case not as a subject but as an example, where the explosive contin-
uum of normality is demonstrated; death, on which the theatre of
the individual is based—in tragedy by its transfiguration, in comedy
by its suppression—is grasped here as a function of life, as production, as one form of labour among others, both organized by and
organizing the collective. FOR ANYTHING NEW TO COME
SOMETHING MUST DISAPPEAR FEAR IS THE FIRST FORM
OF HOPE TERROR IS THE FIRST APPEARANCE OF THE
NEW. A precondition to any performance before an audience is that
the audience be allowed to control both the performance through
the text and the text through the performance, either by sharing in
reading the part of the Chorus, or the part of the first player (A), or

1 Literally, 'learning play', a radical form of political theatre. See the Introduction.

the part of the Chorus by one group of spectators and the part of the first player by another, which would leave unidentifiable the parts that aren't supposed to be shared, or by other means; that is, it can be performed if the reaction of the audience is controlled by an asynchronicity of text and performance, a non-identity of speaker and player. The division of the text given here is a variable schema, and the nature and degree of the variations to be made to it are a political decision, which must be taken from one performance to the next. Variations: the Chorus at certain points provides the first player (A) with someone to play him (A1). All members of the Chorus, either one after the other or simultaneously, perform the part of the first player; while A1 is performing his part, the first player assumes certain parts of the Chorus. No player can take another's part for the entire course of the play. Experiences can only be passed on collectively; training the (individual) capacity to be receptive to experiences is a function of the performance. The second player (B) is played by a member of the Chorus, who resumes his place in the chorus after he has been killed. All props should be used quite openly: objects, costumes, masks and make-up should all be placed on stage. The city of Vitebsk stands for all cities in which the Revolution was, is or will be forced to kill its enemies.THE HORATIAN

PHILOCTETES
THREE POINTS[1]

1

The plot is a model, not a story. It shows positions, not meanings. Every set of events quotes other, similar events from the past, in so far as they have been, and will be, shaped on the Philoctetes model. The siege of Stalingrad quotes Attila's palace on the Danube. (In retrospect it might make more sense to see the latter as quoting the former.) The characters' reflections on events, both cognitive and emotional, also have the character of quotations. The gesture of quoting must not detract from the intensity and spontaneity of their reactions. A feel for the details should coexist with an estrangement from the totality. The German soldiers at the siege of Stalingrad had not learnt the lesson of the Niebelungs. The repetitive nature of the unique event must also be quoted. Only by changing the model can we learn anything from history.

---

1 These remarks on the production of *Philoctetes* were sent to the director Hans Lietzau, who produced the first West German staging of the play at the Munich Residenztheater in 1968. Its performance in the West was considered a provocation by the East German cultural authorities, and Müller was required to send Lietzau these 'Three Points' in order to defuse interpretations of the play as anti-Stalinist. They nevertheless shed some useful light on Müller's intentions in writing it.

2

The Philoctetes model is determined by the class structure of the society presented in it (the army as a function of its general, a relationship that can only be isolated from the dialectic ideologically: by reversing its terms, it can still be sublated) and by the form of property (the weapons, as examples of private property, are elements of the plot, not props).

3

The events need only inevitably take the course they do so long as the system itself is not questioned. Comedy in the performance provokes discussion of what the system presupposes. Only the clown can question the circus. Philoctetes, Odysseus and Neoptolemos: three clowns and gladiators of their own world views.

1968

FAREWELL TO THE LEHRSTÜCK

Dear Steinweg,[1]

I have, with increasing reluctance, been trying to retrieve from the detritus of our discussion of the LEHRSTÜCK (the detritus being my part) something that might be of use to a third party. The attempt has failed; I can think of nothing more to say about the form. In 1957, a certain disciple of Brecht's made this criticism of CORRECTION: the stories aren't aimed at anyone. What isn't aimed at anyone can't be staged. Setting aside the contemptible notion of art and pre-industrial vision of society implied by this, in 1977 I know still less about who I'm writing for than I did back then; today, even more than in 1957, plays are written for the theatre rather than for audiences. I'm not going to sit around twiddling my thumbs until some (revolutionary) situation emerges. But neither am I in the business of speculative theorizing: I'm not a philosopher; I need some determinate reason to make me think; I'm not an archaeologist either, and I've the feeling we may have to bid farewell to the LEHRSTÜCK, at least until the next earthquake hits.

1 Reiner Steinweg (born 1939) is a West German literary critic with a special interest in the Brechtian *Lehrstück*. In 1977 he interviewed Müller for a collection of essays on Brecht's texts intended for use by secondary school teachers. Müller later retracted his interview and wrote instead the following letter to its editor, explaining the reasons for his decision. The letter was then included in the book instead of the interview.

The Christian end times of THE MEASURES TAKEN are over, history has adjourned its street trials, even the trained choirs have stopped singing, Humanism look increasingly like terrorism and the Molotov cocktail has become a way of rounding off a properly bourgeois education. There remain: solitary texts, awaiting history. That, and the leaky memory and fragile wisdom of the masses, both equally threatened by oblivion. When you find yourself amid terrain where LEHRE—the lesson of the LEHRSTÜCK—is so deeply buried, a terrain, indeed, that is mined, you need to stick your head in the sand (mud, stone) every now and then if you're going to see any way ahead. A strategy of burrowing, or constructive defeatism.

4 January 1977

CONVERSATION WITH HEINER MÜLLER
[on PHILOCTETES]

DIETER KRANZ. According to the published edition of the play, you worked on PHILOCTETES from 1958 to 1964, that is, for six years—no doubt not uninterruptedly, but still for a considerable length of time. Then there's a poem of yours written in 1950 that also deals with Philoctetes—that is, from a time before you'd written your first plays. What was it about this mythological figure that so interested and fascinated you?

HEINER MÜLLER. I don't think I can answer the question quite so straightforwardly any more. It was too long ago. If you read the poem I wrote in 1950 that deals with the material for the first time, what strikes me now in retrospect is that it treats Philoctetes' situation somewhat satirically. It's an attempt to subordinate the rights of the individual, represented by Philoctetes, to political and historical necessity. In 1958 or 1964, when I was writing the play, it was no longer possible to treat the matter quite so simply. Of course there are times when the individual's claim to happiness must, let us say, be subordinated to other considerations. But when you get to certain fundamental things, then the subjective factor becomes more and more important, and it's increasingly about the individual—for example, when social conditions are being created.

KRANZ. So by the time you wrote the play, Philoctetes had become for you the incarnation of a victim of injustice.

MÜLLER. No, not necessarily. It's not about morality. It's not about who has committed an injustice against whom. History consists of people who are made the victims of injustices. Otherwise history couldn't happen, would never have happened. And the only question is what attitude you take to that, what conclusions you draw from it. I at any rate think that to shut your eyes to it is to draw the wrong conclusion. But injustice is the wrong word. It's not about looking at or judging things morally.

KRANZ. What is the right word?

MÜLLER. Well, there are different groups of people with different sets of interests, and certain interests assert themselves over other interests.

KRANZ. It's about the interest of the individual against the interest of the community; the individual would in this case be Philoctetes, the community Odysseus and Neoptolemos, representing the Greeks. Would that be right?

MÜLLER. You could more or less put it that way.

KRANZ. So it's about the means by which the community pursues its interests against the individual. In Odysseus' case these are rather distasteful: they involve lies and manipulation. Don't you also make a moral judgement about that?

MÜLLER. I would be very cautious about doing so. Look, I've had some experience with productions of this play in West Germany, for example, and in the West in general. They all had one thing in common: the director never knew how to deal with the character of Odysseus. He was always a bad guy, a straightforward villain and manipulator, who was portrayed as a cynical or even diabolical figure, cynically manipulating this noble youth; and I consider that a very unpolitical and bourgeois view to take—to see history or politics in moral terms. I think that's a bourgeois attitude to history. And the question of means is also a practical question. Every interest group will use the means necessary to pursue its interests.

KRANZ. So Schiller's question of whether a good cause can ennoble evil means is irrelevant? Or should it simply be answered in the affirmative?

MÜLLER. I think it's the wrong way of putting the question.

KRANZ. If it's the wrong way of putting the question, what does the collision between the interests of the individual and the interests of the community amount to?

MÜLLER. I think we shouldn't get bogged down by the question just because we're talking about the play. We're talking about a play that gets performed and that therefore happens in the presence of an audience. It's performed on stage for people sitting in an auditorium and I think you can only really interpret plays in that context. Of course, a play like PHILOCTETES is also aimed at provoking audiences, and the audience has to react to its provocation. I think that one danger of the interpretations (and criticisms) we make of it is that they always leave the audience out, that they judge a play as something that begins and ends on stage—and is only relevant to the stage. But drama can only take place between the stage and the auditorium.

KRANZ. Sure, but the author sets out to tell his story from a certain position. It must be possible to identify that position.

MÜLLER. I think that's also a myth. That formulation contains a simplification that simply isn't true. We've got used to it, but it simply isn't true. First of all, it's not entirely certain that an author's texts directly convey his intentions. An author can have a quite different intention to the one he conveys. He can write something that doesn't reflect his intentions at all, whether he knows it or not.

KRANZ. That's the famous Balzac effect . . .

MÜLLER. Yes. Otherwise writing wouldn't be a form of praxis. Otherwise it too would be entirely parasitic. If you could precisely relate a thing to intentions and results, and measure which of the intentions have come out in the results and which not, then computers could write plays. I think it is still open to question whether computers can do that.

KRANZ. Of course there's no doubt that, looked at objectively, a work of art always contains more than just its author's intentions. Nevertheless, there is still such a thing as the author's intentions.

MÜLLER. Hm . . .

KRANZ. They must nevertheless be identifiable.

MÜLLER. Well, but the author's intentions aren't, generally speaking, ideological, at least mine aren't . . .

KRANZ. What are they then?

MÜLLER. It's rather hard for me to say. I would really have to lie, I would have to make something up, or start theorizing, if I wanted to tell you now what my intentions were back when I was writing PHILOCTETES. I really could end up thinking about it for a long time. I could tell you any number of things. But they would all be inventions of the moment, perhaps more of my present situation than the one back then, which I can no longer remember very precisely.

KRANZ. You mean, they would be more interpretations from today's point of view than an account of your intentions at the time?

MÜLLER. Lukács has a term, 'fundamental experience', which is far more useful than the concept of 'intention'. Every writer has had a fundamental experience, and it has usually occurred early on in their lives. This experience is their motivation to write. And intentions in the sense that you mean them are something rather superficial. And if I think about my fundamental experience or my motivation, then of course it is the case that in the years up to 1945 I experienced history as something that intruded very directly into my life.

KRANZ. You mean the experience of fascism?

MÜLLER. Yes, and subsequently there were of course other experiences that had to do with politics, which directly intruded into my life in another way. It needn't necessarily be something that is opposed to the individual, but just something that no longer leaves the individual as an individual, or which no longer leaves them a consistent whole. And I think that is the starting point for one's attitude to this kind of history, and for the way in which one tells history anew.

KRANZ. Some reviewers have accused your play of historical pessimism. One of them has this to say, 'I reject the ugly implications of the events this work portrays, I reject the pessimism it articulates so categorically, and expresses in such formally perfect verse, as if humanity were hopelessly and forever trapped in a barbaric Ice Age.' Another reviewer says something similar. He claims that Philoctetes' hatred becomes pure misanthropy. And that the play's progressive condemnation of Odysseus turns into a condemnation of any political action taken in the interests of the state. I read your parable of Philoctetes differently. But how would you respond to the charge of historical pessimism?

MÜLLER. As far as historical pessimism goes, I don't really understand how you can make that kind of accusation of a play about a Greek myth that's being used to offer a negative model demonstrating three false attitudes to reality, to history. How you get from there to historical pessimism I don't know. So I really can't understand the criticism.

It's no secret that the play, which was written roughly between 1958 and 1964, was also an examination of problems and distortions relating, among other things, to the figure of Stalin. As long as you don't specify this, you can't talk about historical pessimism. The first thing you need to do is describe the historical references very precisely. Then you can talk about whether or not it's pessimism. But until you've defined these references precisely, it's simply unfair to formulate such a general accusation

KRANZ. You mentioned that all three characters have a false relationship to a particular historical process. In what way? In what way does each of them act falsely?

MÜLLER. In 1964 a couple of students in West Berlin, I think it was, wanted to do a production of the play. One of them wrote me a very long letter about it, in which he suggested that Odysseus could be played wearing a mask showing Hegel's face, and that Philoctetes could be played in a mask showing Sartre's, that is, as an Existentialist, and that Neoptolemos wouldn't be wearing any mask yet. He still doesn't have any ideology of his own. Odysseus then thrashes one into him. I thought that was a very interesting point to start from. Odysseus behaves pragmatically in the situation he finds himself in; Philoctetes behaves, shall we say, individualistically, to put it very simply; and Neoptolemos is the character with the greatest range of action at the beginning of the play because he doesn't yet have any particular position. And in the course of the story he loses that range of action, has it taken away from him, so that at the end he has the most limited range.

KRANZ. Could the opportunity have arisen in this situation for Neoptolemos to act correctly, to acquire a greater range of action?

MÜLLER. Well, certainly not by the solution proposed by the critic Rainer Kerndl: that Neoptolemos stab Odysseus instead of Philoctetes. The question is very difficult to answer. I know that for a long time while writing it I wasn't sure how it would end. From the beginning it wasn't clear to me how it would end. It wasn't all worked out from the start. There was a classical fragment that hasn't survived. There's only an account of it from Euripides, where the story is that Odysseus and Neoptolemos arrive on the island to persuade Philoctetes to come back with them. And before they do they encounter a group of Trojans who are trying to to get Philoctetes to come back with them.

KRANZ. Was that what gave you the idea? Is that what interested you?

MÜLLER. That was one thing that gave me the idea. In the end it appeared in a different form, in the story that Odysseus invents in order to exploit Philoctetes' death. For a long time I meant to tell the story that way. I no longer remember why I changed my mind. It's hard to say in retrospect. But in any case, these days I think it would have been too simplistic a solution, though it would certainly have been much better received than the one I chose. But it would really have avoided the real issue, and lent the whole thing a very superficial kind of contemporary relevance. Of course, the fundamental issue it raises is undoubtedly very uncomfortable. And I don't know the answer to it either; the fundamental issue is, now as then, that history does not happen without victims, and that you can never say which victim is already one too many. You know that phrase of Lenin's: in a brawl you can never exactly judge which blow was one too few and which one too many. And history is, then as now, a brawl. And it will always be hard to decide which blow was one too many. And you cannot simply shut your eyes to that. That is the point.

1977

LETTER TO THE DIRECTOR OF THE FIRST
BULGARIAN PRODUCTION OF 'PHILOCTETES'
AT THE DRAMA THEATRE, SOFIA

Dear Mitko Gotscheff,[1]

Your production of PHILOCTETES at the Sofia Theatre
helped me to see the play in a new way. By that I don't mean:
it helped me to see it for the first time, since that might be
understood as a mere compliment by critics who have no
other productions to compare it with. There is a set design by
Karl von Appen for a production that was planned for the
Berliner Ensemble. It looks like something from the facade of
the Schönbrunn Palace in Vienna and shows a naked old
man holding a golden bow and sitting atop a mound of black
volcanic rock, while at the front of the stage stand the dele-
gates from the Greek high command at Troy, dressed in ceremonial armour. An anachronistic tableau. I don't need to
tell you that theatre lives by anachronisms. Brechtian histori-
cization is just another name for the collision (the drama) of

---

1 Dimiter Gotscheff (born 1943) directed the first Bulgarian production of
Philoctetes. The play had been banned in Bulgaria on account of its alleged
anti-Stalinism and Gotscheff's production was performed late at night and
in secret, following the end of the officially scheduled play and before an audience that had learned of it through word of mouth. Müller missed the pre-
miere but attended one of the later performances, which left him deeply
moved; he would later consider it a paradigmatic production of his text.

different temporal strata (of the material, of the author, of the actors and of the audience) that determine the context of its life. Schönbrunn stands for the implosion of the Renaissance in the Baroque. The pomp of the facade expresses the hollowing out of values, the great historical movement congeals into the great theatrical entrance, Humanism dons a uniform. The old man on the rock represents exile, the motor and price of progress. The use of ceremonial armour for the mission to Lemnos should reveal how the dazzling brilliance of language can serve as an instrument of domination. (As long as the Nazis were fighting an offensive war, their propaganda films didn't need much dialogue. Capitalism was identical with them, their images spoke for it, its interests determined what was shown. By contrast, dialogue dominates the propaganda films of the Western Allies, whose war with Germany was essentially fratricidal.) Hans Lietzau's production at the Munich Residenztheater presented a kind of circus in which three (bloodstained) clowns belaboured themselves and each other with their different conceptions of the world. But because it didn't organize the body's resistance to the text, the actor playing Odysseus couldn't make his character's tragedy legible. What was missing was the utopian moment, which is preserved in the (poetic) language like an insect in amber. Helene Wiegel considered PHILOCTETES, like Brecht's MEASURES TAKEN, to be unperformable. It lacked the contingent, the inessential, the 'grit'. She didn't see, and perhaps, as an actor of the Brechtian theatre, couldn't see that in plays of this kind (which are shaped by their material—humanity in transition from one epoch to another) the contingent can only be brought into play by the actor, that his body is the grit in which the text simultaneously both inscribes and effaces itself, that it is a substitute for other bodies which have been abandoned to the massacre of ideas, to the lethally factual word that Hölderlin dug out of Sophoclean tragedy only to beat his forehead against it because it could no longer comprehend his present, to the word as fact, to the murder words commit, to the terror that emerges when practice becomes theoretical, like Oedipus' pursuit of the oracle's truth.

I saw this way of translating text into theatre in the physical language of your production at the Sofia Theatre, the transformation of fable from a site of contradictions into an endurance test for the participants, the body's struggle against its violation by the expediency of ideas, the WORD THAT BECOMES MURDER. The total test of endurance that human collectivities have been exposed to in the course of what may be our last century (if resistance runs dry and loses its place between the two polarities) is something humanity can only survive collectively. That basic principle of Communism, ALL OR NOTHING, acquires its definitive meaning in the context of the possible suicide of the entire race. But the first step towards raising the individual into this collectivity is to tear him apart; death or Caesarian birth are the alternatives facing the NEW MAN. Theatre simulates this step, being both the pleasure house and chamber of horrors of transformation. In this sense PHILOCTETES is, in contrast to its fashionably concise interpretation as a drama of disillusionment, the negative image of a Communist play. Georgi Miladinov's Philoctetes has the proud stupidity (STUPID AND PROUD AS EAGLES) of the tragic hero. He makes cleverly inventive use of his injured foot: as ornament, as burden, as bait. And of his identity: when overwhelmed by pain, he becomes its own footnote, a howling commentary upon his diseased limb. The wound can be used as a weapon because the foot marks the hole in the net, the gap in the system, the space for freedom between animal and machine that is forever threatened and must forever be conquered anew, in which the utopia of a human community can be discerned. The limping bird estranges flight. Tragedy runs dry. Its course rejects consolation, which is a merely temporary reprieve. It bears in itself the void, the possible beginning. There are tragic races and peoples. Matthias Langhoff has a story about a fiesta at a village in Yucatan: a rock band came from a nearby town, and for two hours two thousand Indians listened motionless and stony-faced to the Siren music of their enemies. They didn't need to have themselves tied to a mast (in any case, there was almost certainly no one to do this for them) like Odysseus the European, that single-handed creator and destroyer of tragedy. They had been eating death since Columbus. Their whole existence has been determined by the question of who will break their teeth upon whom. The new Rome is called the USA, Che Guevara is the Southern Cross.

Like Jason, the first colonist, who is killed by his own vessel on the threshold between myth and history, Odysseus is a transitional figure. With him, the history of peoples enters the politics of men of action, fate loses its face and becomes the mask of manipulation. Dante projected the point of no return upon the fiery curtain of his INFERNO, Odysseus' wreck off the coast of Atlantis:

> FOR FROM THE NEWFOUND LAND A
>   STORM HAD GROWN
>
> . . .
>
> UNTIL THE SEA HAD CLOSED UP OVER US.

With his grimacing performance, Dimiter Ganev inscribes the split in his character that is the stigma of the transitional figure, and drives him from marmoreal effigy into living role. The border runs through the body that crosses it: the splitting is the act of passage. As the first play-actor of his fate, Odysseus is the eternal stranger, his name No Man, his land No Man's Land. From the deserts sown by his tread a sandstorm rises up against him and perforates Hegel's INGENIOUS GREEK. He will be the first to be able to step out of his skin and learn the chill of estrangement. He will enjoy it. Only occasionally will the set of grimaces that are his face freeze again, as if wanting to withdraw into the enclosed space of the effigy, sealed off from the world and the eyes of men, there to recite the text that has poured forth from the abyss behind the broken paling of his teeth since Homer, blind to the consequences, set his tongue moving.

Neoptolemos remains inside the effigy. He is made of the stuff that monuments are built of. The chapter of his life entitled 'Philoctetes' describes his first step along his journey into petrification, the first roughing out by the sculptor, who is history, of the sculpture, using Odysseus the pragmatist as his tool. The lesson that Operation Lemnos offers its recruit is: blood heals wounds. If the effigy cracks, its joints will be smeared with blood. Blood will be his second skin. When it has dried, the monument will be complete. In contrast to Philoctetes, torn and rent, he embodies the patched-together self-confidence that the experience of violence transforms into aggression. Aided by his costume, something between Stone and Space Age, reptilian armour and astronaut's suit, his body shuddering from the convulsions of puberty as if from the pangs of labour, like one enacting the birth of death, becoming his own answer to life's unconquered disorder, Ivailo Gerasov depicts the trembling outline of the heraldic figure of the warrior from HAMLET's play-within-a-play, which describes Neoptolemos' descent (here transformed into Pyrrhus) into the notoriety of the first butcher at Troy, a request performance for intellectuals who can't stand the sight of blood but still like tasting it:

> The rugged Pyrrhus, he whose sable arms,
> Black as his purpose, did the night resemble
> When he lay couched in th'ominous horse,
> Hath now this dread and black complexion smear'd
> With heraldry more dismal: head to foot
> Now he is total gules, horridly trick'd
> With blood of fathers, mothers, daughters, sons,
> Bak'd and impasted with the parching streets,
> That lend a tyrannous and a damned light
> To their lord's murhter. Roasted in wrath and fire,
> And thus o'er-sized with coagulate gore,
> With eyes like carbuncles, the hellish Pyrrhus
> Old grandsire Priam seeks. —Anon he finds him
> Striking too short at Greeks. His antique sword,
> Rebellious to his arm, lies where it falls,
> Repugnant to command. Unequal match'd,
> Pyrrhus at Priam drives, in rage strikes wide,
> But with the whiff and wind of his fell sword
> Th' unnerved father falls. Then senseless Ilium,
> Seeming to feel this blow, with flaming top
> Stoops to his base, and with a hideous crash
> Takes prisoner Pyrrhus' ear; for lo his sword,

Which was declining on the milky head
Of reverend Priam, seem'd i' th' air to stick.
So as a painted tyrant Pyrrhus stood
And, like a neutral to his will and matter,
Did nothing.
But as we often see, against some storm,
A silence in the heavens, the rack stand still,
The bold winds speechless, and the orb below
As hush as death, anon the dreadful thunder
Doth rend the region; so after Pyrrhus' pause,
A roused vengeance sets him new a-work,
And never did the Cyclops' hammers fall
On Mars' armour forg'd for proof eterne
With less remorse than Pyrrhus' bleeding sword
Now falls on Priam.
Out, out, thou strumpet Fortune! All you gods,
In general synod take away her power!
Break all the spokes and fellies from her wheel,
And bowl the round nave down the hill of heaven
As low as to the fiends!
But who, ah woe, had seen the mobled queen
Run barefoot up and down, threat'ning the flames
With bisson rheum, a clout upon that head
Where late the diadem stood, and for a robe,
About her lank and all o'er-teemed loins,
A blanket, in the alarm of fear caught up—
Who this had seen, with tongue in venom steep'd
'Gainst fortune's state would treason have pronounc'd,
But if the gods themselves did see her then,
When she saw Pyrrhus make malicious sport
In mincing with his sword her husband's limbs,

The instant burst of clamour that she made,
Unless things mortal move them not at all,
Would have milch the burning eyes of heaven,
And passion in the gods.

The monuments won't blossom before the last battle. I know of no other production of the play that solves its structural problem, which is the transition from tragedy into farce, or into what Schiller called *tragic satire*, and which comes when Odysseus sees beyond the indispensability of the living Philoctetes and grasps how he might still be made use of dead: at this point, a new species, the political animal, makes its appearance on stage. Having proved to be a dud, the miracle weapon must be defused; Odysseus improvises a state funeral for it, then pulls his box of tricks out from behind the scenery and brings out the double, the divisible puppet that will replace the (indivisible) hero. In so doing he offers a glimpse of a future made technically possible by the exchangeability of the individual. The question of whether the box of tricks subtracts the appearance of having been intentional from the outcome of 'events', something politics needs just as badly as the older fate needed to disguise chance as necessity, is the question of the place of theatre in the moment between its material and the representation of that material. The production resolutely defends this against the cannibalism of empathy, against the terror of the concept, the death inflicted by experience. Svetlana Tsvetova's stage design banishes the audience to the stage, the place of exile. Trapped between the surf of the empty auditorium and the machine of the theatre, with the stage's elevator, bridges and rotating platform reserved for the actors' use alone, the audience no longer has any role to play; it has become part of the flotsam of its own history, which the text carves from the frozen sea of its memory. When nihilism becomes the vanishing point of Christian capitalist politics, the hour of the actor tolls. Reference to the other side turns reality into a means to an end, the world into pretext. Theatre will only rediscover its memory for reality when it forgets its audience. The actor's contribution towards emancipating the spectator is his emancipation from the spectator. The dramaturgic consequence of the spatial solution is to place the prologue at the centre of the play, in the space occupied by the spectators, where the antagonists' insight into the contingency of their own enmity can enable them to imagine a different course of events, in contrast to the habit of personalizing conflicts, which is based on the illusion of individuality. The prologue puts the circus itself in question: the ghost of comedy denounces the cunning of reason as the witty rejoinder you only think of when it's too late. The centre of the play is the calm eye of the storm, whose force and magnitude are marked by two revolutions of its outer circumference. The storm revolves slowly while the enraptured young enthusiast delivers his blind eulogy to Ajax's suicide, blind to how the hero had actually stumbled and fallen out of his heroic illusions concerning Operation HELENA. (In his madness, the offended Greek attacks the cattle whose meat sustains the besiegers' fighting strength, taking them for his countrymen, the true calves to the slaughter; this in itself offers a vague outline of an insight that came much later, a blind preview of Euripides' dark vision of the underground garages of history, which he reveals in his tragi-comedy of the Egyptian Helena: following the destruction of Troy, the Greeks have scarcely set sail before Helena, recaptured and bound for home on board Menelaus' ship, dissolves into fiery air. On a stopover in Egypt, the astonished victors encounter the true Helena alive, living inside a temple where she has spent the course of the Trojan war. The *causus belli* had been a phantom, a joke played by malevolent gods.) The novice has consumed his heroes, the ideals to which he had aspired, and dances with the dead, an erotic rite of initiation. The dead propagate themselves by example, pubescent energy feeds the war machine, the youth marches pregnant into battle, with death as an embryo beneath his heart. I recall a scrap of poetry by a rightly forgotten author, who reduced the phenomenon to its common, fascist denominator: WHEN THE HERO ARISES / IN THE SOUL OF THE YOUTH / WIDE-EYED AND SILENT / CERTAIN OF HIS ETERNAL MISSION . . . The eternal nature of the mission is understood as the imperialist dream of unceasing genocide. Goethe's version of the ballad of Erlkönig offers an abiding image of the occupation of the subject as a precondition to its colonisation: O WILT THOU COME AWAY WITH ME FAIR CHILD . . . The second (sudden) revolution of the storm is reserved for the paroxysm of revenge. Philoctetes the exile, reduced to animal being by a political decision, rehearses his return to humanity by forcing the man responsible for his exile to crawl about on all fours. Neoptolemos, who withdraws from circulation what can no longer be integrated into the dominant form of exchange, brings the matter to a point and the storm to a standstill, with its radius for action at its widest extent because its horizon is at its most narrow. Part of the production's realism is its insistence, by its use of props, on the reality of theatre. Another reality, such as that of the audience or of history, is not simulated. The box for the double corresponds to the glass display case for the bow. The latter is used only once as a weapon, to kill Philoctetes, and, to extend the image of war into the play's present, as a parody of a submachine gun. Exhibiting the bow as a museum piece or a relic prepares the way for Odysseus' chilling insight that the use-value of the dead official is no lower than what he'd be worth alive, and quite possibly greater, so long as the army is the property or function of the general. The first excavation: birth of archaeological thinking. (One consequence of archaeology, and the possible final product of Humanism as the emancipation of human beings from their dependence on nature, is the neutron bomb.) The state's appropriation of the dead man reveals a Roman side to Sophocles, who revises the story in the light of a vision of the Trojan war as history's bloody detour on its way towards the founding of Rome, the event that will bring the age of Greece to an end. The contemporary parallel: Hitler's attack on the Soviet Union and the manner in which it produced the opposite result to the one intended, opening up the capitalist world for the shock wave of the third, driven IN THE NAME OF THE ACROPOLIS and triggered by the October Revolution. The continuation of colonialist politics by means of development aid is gathering the potential to overthrow the system. The spiral of history is laying waste the centres by grinding them down from the peripheral zones. It is this process, which is making the future seem increasingly meaningless to an entire generation, that gives reason for doubt in any progress. It will remain existential as long as humanity does not develop a new species-consciousness, whose precondition is the possibility of a universal history. The loss of this was the price that had to be paid for leaving the animal world. Trying to find a way back is a romanticism of the noble savage, the modern attempt at diverting the course of the spiral into an orbit, and its consequence will be the destruction of the planet.

While I write this, I have before me a Renaissance picture: it shows two saddled horses, standing alone in a broad courtyard bounded by Romanesque architecture. Pawing the flagstones with their hooves, which produce nothing but dust invisible to the human eye, rubbing their necks against each other, they await their riders, who have perhaps already been killed or have killed each other in one of the inner courtyards. When the discotheques have been abandoned and the academies deserted, we will once again hear the silence of the theatre, which is the basis of its language.

27 March 1983

CONVERSATION WITH DRAMA STUDENTS ON
'THE HORATIAN'

HEINER MÜLLER. It was really Johanna's idea to do THE HORATIAN together with THE SCAB . . .[1]

JOHANNA SCHALL.[2] Well it occurred to me for really rather pragmatic reasons. I thought we could do a sort of parallel matinée with the women, which is so popular here right now. And because I think that they're both really about the same thing, or at least about how the effects of an individual's behaviour are always heavily determined by circumstances,

1 *The Scab*, written in 1957–58 (German title: *Der Lohndrücker*), was Müller's first play and an instant success. Among its various themes, the play highlighted how the newly founded Socialist state was frequently dependent on former supporters of Fascism. Balke, the 'scab' of the title, was an informer during the war who handed over a Communist saboteur to the Nazi authorities. But the same motivation for material gain makes him willing to make himself equally useful under the new regime. His actions quickly provoke the hostility of his fellow workers.

2 Johnna Schall (born 1958) is a German actress and director, and the granddaughter of Bertolt Brecht. At the time of this interview she was an actor at the Deutsches Theater in East Berlin.

and about how those circumstances determine whether that behaviour is judged to be good or bad. That's what you find in THE SCAB, and that's also what you find in THE HORATIAN. I first read it when I was 14, and I remember feeling rather sceptical about these enormously sensible decisions that the masses take, I remember thinking that the decisions people take aren't as sensible as the ones they make in the play. For me that became clear when they come to understand the threat posed by the Etruscans, who come up again and again throughout the text, every 10 lines there's something about the Etruscans, how they're a constant threat and how they're up to their necks in shit, and how for that reason they suddenly become quite sensible. If the threat were lifted, they'd all just start killing each other, but as it is the pressure's there. And at the time I thought that you could do it in front of the Iron Curtain, and have the threat that's constantly there coming from this third enemy who's lowering behind the Iron Curtain, and that somehow, whenever they're mentioned or something like that, you have noise or light, so that you can clearly see why it is that everyone is being so smart and left-wing. And then I also thought that both the people who die could be the same person, if only because they're both the ones who are dead at the end. Why they've been killed lies in the eye of the beholder, whether the killing was justified, carried out in order to win the war, or whether it was committed out of passion or delusion, the point is that both of them are dead. The Horatian does the same thing each time, he kills someone, the only difference is the way the killing is judged. And that really is a question that comes up very often, namely whether it really is so easy to make these kinds of judgements, since the dead stay dead. And the father's really the worst, he's such a dreadful old Nazi . . .

MÜLLER. Why is he a Nazi?

SCHALL. Well, to begin with he's, on the face of it, someone who sees his daughter lying dead on the ground and then starts cheering wildly that his son is a war hero. I found that, shall we say, somewhat questionable. His justification that he's only got his son now is all very well, but he gets over the fact that he's lost a child pretty damn fast. And he's also the one who holds out against the people's decision to the end, and keeps on saying that you can't judge him because he's won this victory for us. He's the kind of person who'll be cheering on the war right to the very end, right on till everything is destroyed, someone who'll still be saying we should shoot with the atom bomb hanging over our heads.

MÜLLER. What do you think, you've read it as well.

STUDENT 1. The first time I read it, I initially thought of it in rather narrow terms, in terms of the cult of Stalin. Because for me the figure of Stalin, someone who really led the campaign for industrialization, which nevertheless also cost an incredible number of lives . . . I saw that in the character of the Horatian in this play. Then it went beyond that, but I still primarily saw it in terms of political leaders.

STUDENT 2. I also saw it that way when I first read it. But then I tried to see it in more general terms, also in relation to THE SCAB. The Horatian as the hero, because he's won this battle, and Rome rules over Alba. Like anyone, this hero has two sides to him, it's just that in this case they're fairly extreme. Perhaps not every hero does what he does, but they might perhaps cause other people to die simply by their use of words. And you can't then just point to them and say, that's a hero. That's what struck me.

STUDENT 3. What mattered most to me was the way the people, the masses, saw things. The categorical way they describe their differences. Some of them say he is an absolute victor, others that he's an absolute loser.

SCHALL. I think there's quite a funny point in the play. If you read the whole thing, it's quite logical up to about five lines before the end. Then suddenly you get: 'An example of pure division for the future / not hiding the remainder . . .'. The phrase is just slipped in, so that you might almost miss it. And I think, and I don't mean this badly, Heiner, but it almost comes across as precocious, it makes you think, that's true; but it just can't be entirely true. I think this phrase is key to understanding what's happened up till then. Usually things aren't as simple as they appear here. It would be nice if things could be decided by a Yes or a No, and in the end everyone came to the same opinion . . .

STUDENT 2. But they don't all come to the same opinion; it's just that they acknowledge both opinions.

STUDENT 3. It's also interesting that the Horatian must have this extreme view of how things ought to be, if he places his supposed love for Rome before everything else. Like killing his sister and then just saying, if you don't love Rome then you've got to die.

STUDENT 4. That's already clear when he kills the Curiatian.

STUDENT 1. For me it also has a specific historical relevance, like for example . . . 'My bride is Rome', that happened quite often in East Germany, when relatives disowned each other; mothers would disown their children because they really did only owe their love to Rome. In general people claim to love both, but there's actually a very big difference between the two.

SCHALL. It also strikes me that the language uses a lot of repetitions, particular formulations, but when you look at history then sometimes it's difficult not to get the impression, even if you're not philosophically trained, that there are certain things that repeat themselves in human history. It has something of the quality of an eternally rotating wheel, and every generation makes it turn in its own way.

MÜLLER. I don't know.

SCHALL. I have a question. If, as the party secretary says, Balke in THE SCAB was a quality controller during the Nazi period because he wanted to be seen as a good worker, and later on he does the same job in different circumstances, and that's something commendable, then . . . he does the same thing, but the circumstances in which he does it change how that thing is judged. That's putting it a bit crudely, but that would be the connection.

STUDENT 4. For me, there's the same problem after the war, when some people are calling Balke a hero because he's raised the norm and brings in 40 per cent, and others are saying he's the bad guy because he's keeping everyone's wages down.

SCHALL. Who is using him as a hero is also an important question.

STUDENT 4. I see the same conflict there as in THE HORATIAN. But I think the thing about the Nazi is interesting. I mean, I haven't read anything so naively for some time.

SCHALL. I might have thought of some other terms to describe him.

STUDENT 4. No, I just mean that we've found a term to describe the father. I wouldn't have known how to deal with him.

MÜLLER. Why, he's got a perfectly good reason. What's wrong with the father or his position?

SCHALL. I just saw it from the point of view of this basic situation. So let's say I'm the sister and I'm dead. My brother has just killed me, and my father comes along and says, oh shit, her brother was so great just now. You should make him a hero now because he fought for you, and you really can't criticize him for doing a bit of slaughtering around here. That would make me feel, if I were still in a position to feel it, a trifle neglected. Either that, or the father is an utter pragmatist, which amounts to the same thing.

MÜLLER. But the fact is the sister *is* dead.

STUDENT 2. He can't really argue for his son to be punished. All he can really do is go out and shoot himself. He doesn't have any alternative.

SCHALL. Who's to know that the son won't turn the next corner, and someone else will say something he doesn't like, and he'll chop his head off. That can also become a habit, that's what you saw with Stalin. If you get away with it the first time, then you'll start doing it left, right and centre.

STUDENT 3. The other thing is . . . of course, what happened to his daughter . . . it's an entirely practical consideration of the father's to do what he can to protect his son.

SCHALL. Well, quite. He gives his son the opportunity to continue expressing this opinion that he's already very clearly expressed. And the Horatian will keep on killing anyone who says anything or just opens their mouth. How marvellous.

STUDENT 3. It's just that I find 'Nazi' such an extreme term . . .

SCHALL. Like I say, there are other words you could use.

STUDENT 1. Well look, to me it seems to be natural for a father to try to protect his own flesh and blood.

STUDENT 2. I think that if the son hadn't killed his own sister, but someone else, it doesn't matter who, then it would be perfectly human and logical for the father to try and save his son who's committed a murder. But since he's killed his own flesh and blood, then there's no real opportunity for him to do the right thing. He can't defend his son, and he can't condemn him. All he can really do is go home and take an overdose. I think an overdose would be the human thing to do.

SCHALL. All right, let's assume he does it out of fatherly feelings, because he thinks that that way he'll have at least one child left. But the arguments that he uses in this situation are really extremely militant. Maybe I can understand that they come out of the exceptional circumstances, but he uses arguments that would make this young guy into a public hero. Even if the motivation behind it is fatherly love, the consequences are pretty dangerous. Aren't they?

MÜLLER. I don't know.

STUDENT 1. All of them do what the father does, except for the daughter. All these characters put politics before human relationships.

STUDENT 3. The Curiatian doesn't. I think that the Curiatian would have been ready to let him live if . . .

SCHALL. No. I think if it had been the other way round the play would just have been called *The Curiatian*. Neither the Etruscans, the Romans, nor the people from Alba have an awful lot of regard for each other. In any case, I don't see how some of them are better than the others or fundamentally different.

MÜLLER. What does this tell us? I don't know. These are all questions . . . but the point is the questions and not the answers. I'm really not here to give answers to things. I can only pose questions, and I don't have any answers. All you can really do with literature and theatre is pose questions and not give answers. Perhaps just to touch on the history of the material, it begins with . . . The story comes from Livy, and is one of the founding myths of Rome. In it there are 10 Horatians and 10 Curiatians, and they kill each other, and the last one kills the man who's betrothed to his sister, and then kills the sister as well because she's so unpatriotically upset by what he's done. So the events of the story are the same, except for the fact it's been reduced to two. And then they hold a trial in the same way and with the same outcome, and the compromise they come up with effectively founds Roman law, which still serves as the basis for European law today. And the compromise is that they build a gate, the gate of the Horatii, and the Horatian goes through it with his face covered, and the father pays a fine—in other words, class justice. The Horatian is needed, and that is the main point here—that he's actually needed, both the young man and the money. Then there's a play by Corneille, in other words, from the period of the French monarchy before the Revolution, and in it the father offers himself as substitute victim for the son. The offer is accepted, and the father is executed instead of the son, because he is not as useful to society as the son—in other words, the monarchist solution. And what we have here now proposes another alternative.

SCHALL. What does the story mean to you?

MÜLLER: I wrote it just after the events in Prague, that is, in 1968, and you can, if you like, read it against that background. So if there are conflicts in a country that's threatened from outside, then you need to talk about them openly and make sure that the external threat is warded off. You need to talk about everything because if you don't, then it looks as if you'll get by better that way, but at the next opportunity things will fall apart all the more surely. And the other thing that I imagined was that it couldn't really be played by adults. It's really a play for children, children playing politics. And politics consists precisely of intimidating, lying and cheating. It is in, other words, the art of the possible, and has nothing to do with truth. It's somewhat exaggerated, but it is politics as it would be conducted by children.

SCHALL. How does the direct popular involvement come into it, something that we're not so used to, because in a case like this we'd be asking ourselves . . .

MÜLLER. It was a primitive polity, early Rome. Things were still like that. There were certainly slaves, who weren't, of course, allowed to take part in debates, but neither did they appear at them. That's how it still is in most societies. Politics is restricted to those who can pay their taxes and everyone else is the object of politics, not a political actor. The other point that is perhaps interesting is the end of the distinction between war and civil war. I mean, one way of looking at it is that there are no longer any civilians. Another is that the distinction still exists. And the end of this distinction begins with the French Revolution, above all, with the idea of revolution itself. Revolution means the end of civilian status, and the consequence of revolution is total war. Before then, there was no concept of total war; war was a duel between armies. And since the French Revolution, in other words, since the advent of people's armies there are no longer any civilians, and that is a problem we're still facing. These are all aspects . . . there's an interesting text where some Germans are talking about life and a Spanish migrant worker says, life is radial in form. You can't restrict it to a single line. And I think we just have to find out what kind of rays emerge from what we do. The only idea I have is very general . . . we just have to start working. I don't have any idea about how the parts should be allocated and I wouldn't like to do that in advance. We have to let it emerge. The only idea I have is that it should in some way be an uninterrupted text. In terms of drama, you can't compare it directly with THE SCAB. We need to keep play and content separate here, not completely neutralize or dissolve the content in the play.

(Pause.)

MÜLLER. Which of you weren't reminded of Stalin when reading the play?

STUDENT 5. Almost all your plays make me think of Stalin.

MÜLLER. He's also very important to me . . .

(Pause.)

SCHALL. Yesterday or the day before there was this broadcast where Gorbachev arrived in the United States and they all sat down together and called each other by their first names, and Gorbachev sang a song . . . That really looked so much like the end of history, everyone being nice to everyone else because they have to be, because there's no alternative. Like a fairy tale or a daydream, don't you think?

MÜLLER. What you don't see at these summit meetings on television is that they all have blood on their hands, like in THE HORATIAN.

SCHALL. But you know it when you're watching the television.

MÜLLER. You don't see the blood on television. That's the difference.

SCHALL. Still, the ending is one that you'd like to see but seldom do.

MÜLLER. But they still have blood on their hands.

SCHALL. And then they shake each others' hands.

MÜLLER. But the blood doesn't come off.

1987

Translator's Note

It was Müller's practice to capitalize the titles of his plays and novels mentioned in his texts (both of his own and other people's), and we have followed this form of notation in these translations. In the texts in this volume not written by Müller—the Introduction and the footnotes—we follow the more usual convention of printing titles in lower case italics.